LANGUAGE AND LITE

Dorothy S. Strickland,
Celia Genishi and Donna E. Alv

ADVISORY BOARD: Richard Allington, Kathryn Au, Bernice
Carole Edelsky, Shirley Brice Heath, Connie Jue

(continued)

For volumes in the NCRLL Collection (edited by JoBeth Allen and Donna E. Alvermann) and the Practitioners Bookshelf Series (edited by Celia Genishi and Donna E. Alvermann), as well as a complete list of titles in this series, please visit www.tcpress.com.

Reading and Representing Across the Content Areas

A CLASSROOM GUIDE

Amy Alexandra Wilson

Kathryn J. Chavez

Foreword by Marjorie Siegel

TEACHERS COLLEGE PRESS

Teachers College, Columbia University
New York and London

Published by Teachers College Press, 1234 Amsterdam Avenue, New York, NY
10027

Library of Congress Cataloging-in-Publication Data

Wilson, Amy Alexandria.
  Reading and representing across the content areas : a classroom guide / Amy
Alexandra Wilson, Kathryn Chavez ; foreword by Marjorie Siegel.
    pages cm
  Includes bibliographical references and index.
    ISBN 978-0-8077-5567-9 (pbk.)—ISBN 978-0-8077-5571-6 (hardcover)—
  ISBN 978-0-8077-7319-2 (ebook)
    1. Content area reading—United States. 2. Language arts—Correlation with
content subjects—United States. I. Chavez, Kathryn. II. Title.
    LB1050.455.W55 2014
    428.4071'2—dc23

                                                                2014005970

ISBN 978-0-8077-5567-9 (paper)
ISBN 978-0-8077-5571-6 (hardcover)
ISBN 978-0-8077-7319-2 (ebook)

Printed on acid-free paper

Manufactured in the United States of America

21 20 19 18 17 16 15 14   8 7 6 5 4 3 2 1

Contents

Foreword

Language occupies a privileged place in classrooms. Even when studying science and social studies—where knowledge is represented by graphs, diagrams, and maps as well as written language—alternatives to talk- and text-heavy teaching practices are rare. The seeming inevitability of language as a tool for learning makes it difficult for many teachers to imagine what multimodal texts and practices could contribute to content area teaching and learning. Fortunately, the publication of *Reading and Representing Across the Content Areas: A Classroom Guide* by Amy Alexandra Wilson and Kathryn Chavez is perfectly timed to set imaginations in motion by showing how multimodality works in different disciplines, what it looks and sounds like in content-area classrooms, and why it matters.

Multimodality—the social practice of making meaning by combining multiple semiotic resources—has taken the field of literacy education by storm. A quick glance at professional journals and conference programs reveals a growing awareness that youth are immersed in a multimodal world and brings knowledge of how to combine different symbolic resources to their participation in social spaces near and far. Despite the profession's enthusiasm, there is a striking absence of attention to multimodality in school. And when multimodality *is* included, it is often considered a curricular frill to motivate students rather than a basis for understanding. Trivializing multimodality in this way not only discounts the essential role multiple representations play in fields such as science, history, and mathematics, but also treats multimodality as a generic or universal practice that works the same way regardless of purpose and context.

Wilson and Chavez start from a completely different premise, one that situates multimodal representations within a discipline. Disciplines are commonly thought of as bodies of knowledge untethered from the circumstances that produce knowledge. In school, they become "school subjects" that treat knowledge as if it were a flat factual statement (usually in a textbook) rather than an artifact of lively debates over appropriate modes of inquiry and the resulting truth value of knowledge claims. In short, *disciplines* are discourse communities and *multimodal representations* are what they argue over. Multimodality will remain a trivial pursuit in classrooms unless it is positioned as the pivot point for understanding disciplinary knowledge as mediated by signs, not a mirror of reality.

Reading and Representing Across the Content Areas: A Classroom Guide is a breakthrough book that will change the conversation about multimodality in content area teaching. In showing how different disciplines tap semiotic resources to represent the world and how teachers seamlessly incorporate these resources into instructional practices, Wilson and Chavez convince us that developing multimodal representational competence matters. Knowing how knowledge is produced and represented provides students with an insider view that challenges the elitism that can leave them standing on the outside. Firsthand experience with the modes, tools, texts, and talk that disciplinary discourse communities employ to learn about the world will not by itself provide access, but it may inspire students to view knowledge and themselves differently.

In bringing together what have been disparate lines of scholarship—multimodality, disciplinary literacy, critical literacy, classroom discourse, and content area teaching and curriculum—Wilson and Chavez make a unique contribution to the field just in time for the challenges posed by the Common Core State Standards. Teachers, teacher educators, and university-based scholars will find rich rewards in the classrooms vignettes and detailed analyses of the teachers' multimodal practices and representations across four distinct content areas: earth science, English language arts, mathematics, and social studies. This is the best kind of classroom guide, one that offers examples and images to ponder and transform rather than a list of "best practices" to implement. One of the hidden gems is the repeated focus on how to talk about multimodality. There is a need for us to expand our own multimodal representational competence, and this includes learning how to talk about multimodal choices and meanings in ways that make visible the semiotics of the discipline, or what different signs stand for in a disciplinary discourse community. Language can continue to be a productive pedagogical resource when it stops serving solely as a channel for transmitting knowledge and becomes one among many ways to represent knowing and learning. In the classrooms that we enter in this book, multimodality has toppled language from its privileged position, but words remain an important part of the multimodal mix.

Marjorie Siegel

CHAPTER 1

Introduction

In a 6th-grade classroom four students sit together at a mineral center, reading the instructions that direct them to scratch samples of calcite and fluorite with a copper penny and a steel nail. They record their observations, noting which mineral is harder, then read Mohs Hardness Scale in their textbooks in order to compare the calcite and fluorite to other minerals. After rotating to the next center, the students test the property of *streak* by sliding hematite and pyrite across a white ceramic tile, recording their observations, and reading a brief section in their textbooks about streak.

In a different classroom a teacher introduces the concept of *style* by displaying a photograph of a character from a popular television show and asking students to notice her distinctive clothes that were designed to "grab your attention." She continues, "We all have different styles, don't we? For example, I love how Sarah [points to student] dresses. I think Sarah has style. But is my style the same as Sarah's?" After students briefly analyze different styles in clothing, famous paintings, and popular songs, they identify stylistic differences in short stories. They then write their own letters using the voice and style of fictional characters they had read about.

Another class consisting of 8 boys and 16 girls lines up on either side of the hallway as part of a larger discussion about ratio. "We can see our ratio, 8 to 16," the teacher says. "Now if we wanted to use everybody and make even groups, is there a way we can do that?" A student responds, "Divide the boys into two groups of 4," and the teacher rejoins, "Okay, if we divided the boys into two groups of 4, how many girls would need to be in each group?" Students rearrange their bodies accordingly, with boys dividing themselves into two groups of 4 on the right side of the hall, and girls standing directly across from them in two groups of 8 on the left side of the hall. Individuals name other groupings they could make—2 to 4, 1 to 2, 8 to 16—and they again rearrange their bodies accordingly. They record the different types of groupings in a table, after which students note patterns in the data such as "every numerator is half of the denominator," and "they're all equivalent to 1 over 2."

In yet another classroom 8th-graders synthesize information across a variety of sources, including statistical displays related to contemporary social issues and videos of people sharing their firsthand experiences with those issues. They then select a contemporary U.S. senator whom they want to portray, or *embody*, for a day; wearing a nametag and dressing as that senator, they will hold a senate debate in which they read arguments they have prepared that try to persuade their colleagues to vote for or against proposed legislation on those social issues.

WHY PROVIDE DISCIPLINARY LITERACY INSTRUCTION ON MULTIPLE REPRESENTATIONS?

As these examples illustrate, as part of learning across the disciplines, students interact with a variety of representations as they manipulate the physical world, listen to music, embody a historical figure, rearrange their bodies in space, interpret patterns in numeric tables, view photographs, or participate in a wide array of related activities. Instead of being peripheral add-ons to learning, multiple forms of representation are often central to reaching disciplinary goals.

In fact, research (e.g., Prain & Tytler, 2012; Wilson, 2010) indicates that some teachers use nonprinted forms of communication—such as gestures, demonstrations, images, or videos—just as often or more often than they use written communication. This finding would suggest that literacy instruction on printed texts, such as teaching students to apply comprehension strategies as they read textbook sections, is important but not sufficient for helping them make sense of disciplinary content that is presented across a wide variety of media.

Moreover, many adolescents now spend over 7 hours per day interacting with some type of media, often on computer or mobile phone screens (Kaiser Family Foundation, 2010). These media are profoundly multimodal in the sense that they incorporate music, moving images and graphs, verbal speech, written text, and so forth. Consequently, several scholars have argued that disciplinary literacy instruction can include helping students understand a wide array of multimodal texts—ranging from novel data visualizations to interactive historical timelines—in order to prepare them for the types of disciplinary texts they will encounter online.

Just as it is important to support students' interpretations of multiple representations, so, too, is it important to assist their production of multiple representations. One compelling reason for teaching students how to produce multiple representations is that this approach often enriches students' understandings. In the words of Marjorie Siegel (1995), "translating meanings from one sign system to another increases students' opportunities to engage in generative and reflective thinking because students must invent connections between the two sign systems" (p. 455). For example, when students take information from a graph and present it verbally and numerically, or when they transform a literary work to an embodied performance, or when they otherwise create multiple forms of representation in regard to the same concept, then they adopt different ways of processing that concept.

Prain and Tytler (2012) have argued that these multiple representations "productively constrain" students' understandings by forcing them to think about disciplinary concepts in particular ways (p. 2751). For instance, viewing Civil War photographs can promote one set of understandings, such as empathetic views of the human toll of the war, but asking students to place the depicted events in a timeline supplements empathetic understandings by situating these events within a constrained chronological framework. As a second example, students may write about the causes of lunar eclipses, but asking them to produce an image adds further constraints to possible "meanings" of this statement by committing specific spatial orientations, sizes, and distances of the earth, moon, and the sun onto paper. In sum, multiple representations both enhance and productively limit how students understand a given disciplinary concept (Ainsworth, 1999).

As Hubber, Tytler, and Haslam (2010) argued, "The demand to explore, generate, and refine representations constitutes a demand to think deeply about the [discipline] itself, and the coordination of representations in constituting explanations and claims is central to the learning process" (p. 25). In accordance with the idea that instruction with and on multiple representations enhances disciplinary learning, the purpose of this book is to outline ways in which content area teachers can provide explicit literacy instruction that supports students in understanding and producing a variety of representations.

These representations are unique to each discipline. Much as written texts exhibit discipline-specific patterns (Lee & Spratley, 2010), we argue that images, embodied representations, and other "texts" exhibit discipline-specific patterns as well. That is, social studies teachers are likely to choose a different set of representations with a different set of features than earth science teachers, and so on. Accordingly, our description of literacy instruction in each discipline is grounded in our previous research on disciplinary gestures (Wilson, Boatright, & Landon-Hays, 2014), images (Wilson & Landon-Hays, in press), and manipulatives/demonstrations (Wilson, 2013), as we describe how literacy instruction can be reconceptualized to account for each discipline's distinctive set of representational features.

Specifically, each chapter in this book addresses one of four disciplines: earth science, English/language arts (ELA), mathematics, and social studies. Within each chapter, we describe several examples of teachers' instruction with and on multiple representations common to that discipline. We then use these instances as springboards for discussing how teachers can enhance their students' understanding of disciplinary concepts through explicit literacy instruction on/with a wide range of printed, digital, embodied, and three-dimensional texts.

WHAT IS A TEXT?

To lay the foundation for these subsequent chapters on literacy instruction, we first describe what we mean by key terms. The first of these terms is *mode,* which can be defined as a "socially shaped and culturally given resource for making meaning" (Kress, 2009, p. 54). Examples of modes include images, gestures, music, three-dimensional models, clothes, spoken words, and written words, each of which is a fully articulated system for making meaning with its own unique structures and forms that can vary depending on the social group that uses it.

For example, men's clothes in Renaissance England were made with a different set of patterns and materials than clothes worn by modern-day baseball players, but in both contexts clothes indicate meaning about the identity of the wearer such as the social groups with which he affiliates. Likewise, written words are structured according to different patterns, such as narratives in English and observations in science, which indicate the goals of people in each discipline. Indeed, many modes—from embodied representations to images—assume discipline-specific forms based on the historical traditions, conventions, and goals of each discipline (O'Halloran, 2005; Rudwick, 1976).

As teachers and students seek to communicate and to solve problems within their disciplines, they often combine modes that most powerfully enable them to convey the aspects of the world that they wish to convey. For example, consider an earth science teacher who wants her students to learn about neap tides and spring tides, which are caused by the gravitational pull of the sun and the moon on the earth as the three celestial bodies align in particular configurations. Because the spatial nature of this relationship is important, a mode that enables the easy viewing of spatial relationships may be the most apt way to convey this physical phenomenon.

In this case, the teacher could assign the roles of earth, sun, and moon to different students, and ask them to move around each other in certain positions while the distant "sun" and the closer "moon" both exert their gravitational pulls on the "earth" by pretending to pull that student toward them. An image such as a diagram is another mode that would enable students to view the spatial relationships between the three bodies at different points in the lunar cycle. Compared to the students' physical actions, an image would convey greater precision in regard to the size, shape, and relative distances among the sun, earth, and moon. Both the diagram and the students' bodies moving through space would enable students to "see" changing spatial relationships—including the different spatial alignment for each type of tide—more quickly and easily than written words (Kress, 2010).

This example points toward the concept of *affordances* (Gibson, 1979; van Leeuwen, 2005), which is based on the premise that different modes lend themselves to representing certain aspects of the world more easily and powerfully than other modes. Images, for example, are governed by the logic of space and consequently afford the visualization of spatial relationships (Kress, 2005). Under this theory, written and spoken language, which have long been focal points in literacy education and related fields (Norris, 2009), are seen as but two means of communication that are best understood as being only part of teachers' and students' communicative repertoires. Students also make sense of various types of images and objects, each of which can be a legitimate and powerful means of expression.

The concept of *affordances* requires definitions of content area texts to be expanded beyond traditional connotations of novels, textbooks, and even websites and apps. Instead, a *text* becomes any instance of communication in any mode or combinations of modes, including those modes that do not appear on a page or on a screen. When text is viewed in this way, content area teachers become text designers who marshal a variety of multimodal resources as they seek effective ways to communicate core disciplinary concepts. Students, too, become text designers who can use body movements, writing utensils, paper and poster board, computers, clay, iPads, objects from the natural world, combinations of clothes, and other materials to build and express their understandings of disciplinary ideas, eventually learning to fashion representations that more closely align with the conventions of each content area.

If concepts of *text* include physical models, embodied representations, and images, then what is the difference between text and representation? For the most part, we use the terms *text* and *representation* almost interchangeably. The term *representation* applies to signs—including written and verbal language, images, gestures, and three-dimensional models—that stand for a referent or that communicate aspects of their referents. These referents might be tangible, such as tectonic plates, or intangible, such as the text-makers' experiences or the products of their imagination.

Sometimes, however, students seek to interpret objects that are not necessarily designed to represent something else, such as clouds or minerals. In his description of archeologists' work, Goodwin (2000) argued that even "*nature*, like any category, is a human semiotic construal" (p. 1513, n. 15) in at least two ways: People use socially generated frameworks for understanding it, and when used in classroom instruction, it often appears with other modes, such as written or verbal explanations (Alvermann & Wilson, 2011). For these reasons, we believe natural phenomena are texts but not necessarily representations.

DISCIPLINARY LITERACY INSTRUCTION AS INSTRUCTION IN REPRESENTATION

Under the assumption that multiple modes can enrich learning in any discipline, we take two approaches to describing how disciplinary literacy instruction can be reconceptualized as guiding students in the interpretation and production of discipline-specific multimodal texts. Specifically, we describe how teachers can support students in these ways:

- Applying *comprehension strategies* to a variety of representations in ways that account for these representations' unique features and each discipline's goals
- Developing *multimodal representational competence*, which includes producing and evaluating a variety of representations that communicate complex disciplinary concepts

Comprehension Strategy Instruction for Disciplinary Representations

For decades, comprehension strategy instruction (CSI) has been a core staple of literacy instruction (Samuels & Farstrup, 2011). It is based on the premise that students who predict and check predictions, make inferences, ask clarification questions, draw connections to other texts, use text features to determine main ideas, summarize, and apply other comprehension strategies can arrive at deeper understandings of disciplinary concepts expressed through texts than students who do not actively engage with texts as they read (Block & Pressley, 2002; see Figure 1.1). Comprehension strategy instruction may also enhance students' ability to engage in difficult content matter by increasing their *metacognition*, the active monitoring and adjusting of their thought processes while reading (Pressley, 2002).

Recent bodies of literature have expanded definitions of disciplinary literacy instruction, arguing that advanced practitioners employ discipline-specific approaches toward texts that include, but extend beyond, these general comprehension strategies (Lee & Spratley, 2010). These approaches include employing discipline-specific criteria for evaluating the quality of texts. Scientists, for instance, often determine whether the authors' claims are based on observable empirical evidence, which includes appraising whether experimental designs are valid and replicable (Shanahan & Shanahan, 2008). Historians, by contrast, do not often evaluate claims in regard to whether they are replicable or generalizable (Becher, 1989), but instead they are concerned with whether other people corroborated them. Additionally, they consider how the group affiliations and self-interests of each author—as well as the context in which each text was written—influenced what was said (Wineburg, 1991).

Mathematicians, too, may consider the self-interested purposes of given authors (Paulos, 1996), but they tend to be more concerned with whether the authors' conclusions logically cohere with accepted postulates and theorems of mathematics. They often seek to detect whether the authors' solutions or explanations include errors such as incompletions or inaccuracies (Shanahan & Shanahan, 2008). Language arts practitioners employ still different criteria for evaluating texts. Often reading texts for aesthetic reasons, they focus on whether or not they enjoy them or evaluate the artistic craft demonstrated by the author (Applebee, 1974; Wineburg & Grossman, 2000). Moreover, readers of literary texts often

FIGURE 1.1. Comprehension Strategies Used by Proficient Readers

Before Reading

Identify a purpose for reading. By themselves or with a teacher, students decide on their purpose for reading. For instance, they may read a textbook section in order to discover how types of rocks are classified or read a poem in order to identify how the author's literary techniques enhanced her or his message.

Make predictions. Readers use their background knowledge and text features to make predictions about the content of the text. Moreover, they may use headings, sub-headings, and other features to determine how a text is organized, such as problem/solution and cause/effect.

During Reading

Identify relevant information. Students distinguish major ideas from minor details. These major ideas are often signified by text features and by the organizational structure of a text. For instance, students may use headings to determine that a text exhibits a cause/effect organizational pattern and then identify the main causes and effects of the French Revolution as they read. Students also distinguish relevant from irrelevant information by noting whether the information helps them meet the purpose they set for reading.

Visualize. As they read, students envision what people, places, or events look, smell, or feel like; they may envision how different categories relate to each other through drawing graphic organizers; or they may visualize patterns or solutions through drawing graphs or pictures.

Make inferences. Readers make conjectures beyond what is explicitly stated in the text, such as inferring why a character may have made a particular decision or how the authors' group affiliations influenced their conclusions.

Ask questions. Readers monitor their comprehension as they read and ask clarification questions when they do not understand aspects of the text. They may consult outside resources, such as websites or their teachers, to help them answer these questions if needed. Readers also may ask critical questions or higher order questions with no clear-cut answers.

Make connections. Students continue the process of activating background knowledge through connecting the text to other texts they have read and to their own experiences. For instance, readers in mathematics may call to mind other problems they have solved similar to the one expressed in this problem, readers in English may compare a character's experiences to their own, and so forth.

After Reading

Summarize. Readers summarize the main ideas of a text in their own words.

Evaluate text. Readers evaluate the text according to different criteria, depending on their purpose for reading. For instance, they may evaluate whether the authors' data were sufficient to prove their point or whether the authors' literary techniques seemed to fit their message.

Confirm, revise, or reject predictions. Readers decide whether, or to what degree, their predictions were correct. They may decide to consult additional texts if their purpose for reading was not met.

Note: Although these strategies are presented as occurring before, during, and after the reading process, readers often apply multiple strategies in recursive, non-linear ways as they read.

empathize with difficult decisions faced by characters as they consider the ethical implications for situations in their own lives (Fernandez, 1977).

Drawing from these current bodies of literature on general comprehension instruction and discipline-specific comprehension instruction, this book describes how students may apply similar types of strategies as they construct understandings across a variety of disciplinary representations, ranging from three-dimensional objects to digital images. We also describe how these strategies can be modified according to the physical characteristics of different types of representation in relation to the goals of each discipline.

Multimodal Representational Competence Across Disciplines

Disciplinary learning has never been just about written texts; students have always interpreted a variety of modes as they constructed understandings of disciplinary concepts. However, an increasing emphasis on digital technologies—ranging from apps on mobile devices to manipulatives on interactive whiteboards—has recently sparked a growing interest in multimodality (Jewitt, 2006). *Multimodal representational competence* (MRC; Yore & Hand, 2010) is a skill that can help students in interpreting and producing multimodal texts, ultimately arriving at deeper understandings of core concepts in each discipline.

MRC, as described throughout this book, derives from theories of representational competence (Kozma & Russell, 1997) and metarepresentational competence (diSessa, 2004). Students develop and exhibit aspects of *multimodal representational competence* as they engage in the following six actions:

(1) Use specific features of representations to support claims, inferences, and/ or predictions. In her social studies class Alice sought to support her students in developing this aspect of MRC when she asked her students to make inferences about dominant societal groups' values based on the statues they erected. For instance, her students viewed photographs of Stalin statues at various locations and periods of time, some of which had been defaced. Students used specific features of the representations of Stalin—such as the height of the pedestals or Stalin's clothes—to answer questions such as these:

- What can you infer about Stalin as a leader through viewing the statues he erected?

- What characteristics did he want others to think he possessed?
- What can you infer about some people's feelings toward his leadership?
- What specific evidence from each photograph supports your assertions?

Just as Alice's students used specific evidence from the photographs to draw inferences about Stalin, students in other disciplines can cite or point toward specific subcomponents of graphs, physical models, diagrams, and other representations, and explain how these subcomponents support their arguments.

(2) Transform one mode to another. Examples of this action include changing a mathematical equation into a three-dimensional solid or a wordless picture book into a written narrative. Grace frequently tried to help her middle school students develop this aspect of MRC when she asked them to translate what they had learned from their science textbook sections into physical models throughout the school year. As one instance of this type of instruction, Grace's students noted areas on their middle school's campus that were eroded, and they asked questions about why it was happening and how they could stop it. As part of this inquiry, they read about soil conservation in their textbooks, which included several photographs of methods that farmers use to minimize the effects of erosion. To test these different methods, Grace poured water on mounds of dirt, which represented hills. The students tried to protect their hills through several measures, such as by shaping them in different ways and by placing cheesecloth and popsicle sticks on them.

In this case, students connected the visual modes of writing and photographs to a more tactile mode that enabled them to manipulate and observe physical effects. Although this type of modal transformation is fairly common to earth science, mode-to-mode transformations vary across disciplines. English/language arts teachers, for instance, may require students to transform scenes from a classic work of literature to visual symbols and drawings (Smagorinsky & O'Donnell-Allen, 1998), whereas mathematics teachers often require students to transform numeric and symbolic representations to a variety of visuals (Brenner et al., 1997). Despite discipline-specific differences in modes, asking students to transform content from one mode to another can enhance their understanding of disciplinary concepts (Wilson, 2012).

(3) Explain the relationship between two or more modes that are used to represent the same phenomenon or communicate the same message. Grace's science students practiced this component of MRC through explaining how their manipulations of dirt related to what they had read in their textbooks. One group of students stated that their cheesecloth represented cover crops and the sticks represented trees, while another group stated that the cheesecloth represented grass and the sticks represented a fence. They also verbally explained how they shaped their dirt to resemble contour plowing and terracing, techniques depicted in their textbook photos. Despite the differences among their verbal explanations, they all articulated that covering the soil, as well as preventing water from moving in a direct path on a steep downhill slope, slowed the process of water erosion caused by the water, which represented rain.

Hagan (2007) noted that the relationship between two modes (e.g., physical models of the hill and the photographs of hills in students' textbooks) can occur on a continuum from "tight" to "loose." Mathematics and science often feature "tight" relationships when the subcomponents of one mode—such as a numeric equation—correspond directly with the subcomponents of other modes, such as an image or three-dimensional model. In Figure 1.2, for example, a net of a rectangular prism (i.e., a pattern that can be folded to make a rectangular prism) is situated next to an equation and the formula for finding the surface area of a rectangular prism. Specific features of the image, such as the lengths and heights of particular rectangles, correspond directly to specific numbers in the equation and letters in the formula. Grace's students explained the relationships between tightly connected modes through point-to-point mapping—that is, through physically pointing to two rectangles in the image and then to their counterpart in the equation—as they explained how they think the two modes "went together."

In other cases, however, modes may be more loosely related, such as the relationship between the physical model of the hill and the photographs in the science textbook. Grace stated that the cheesecloth in the model could have represented multiple items in the photographs, including cover crops or grass.

English and social studies commonly feature loosely related modes as well. For example, Kathryn's students made digital podcasts in language arts, combining music and spoken narratives to represent their experience of a particular event in their lives. In this case, the general tone of the music (upbeat, sad) was selected to represent the general tone of

FIGURE 1.2. In Mathematics, Visual and Numeric/Symbolic Modes Are Often Tightly Related

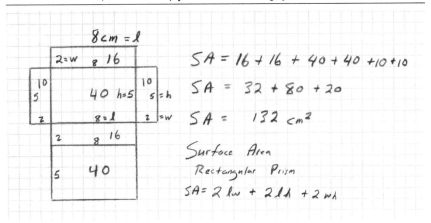

students' experiences without point-to-point correlations among specific notes/bars and words/lines. Like Grace's students, who articulated the relationship between the physical model and the textbook section, Kathryn's students articulated the relationships between the music and their spoken narratives as they explained how the tone of their music related to the tone of their spoken stories. In all, whether the relationships between modes are tight, loose, or somewhere in between, articulating the relationships among them can help students arrive at deeper understandings of what the modes represent, as well as deeper understandings of the communicative practices of each discipline (Hubber et al., 2010; Kozma & Russell, 1997).

(4) Evaluate multimodal representations and explain why a particular representation (or set of representations) is more apt for a particular purpose than other representations. The theory of affordances assumes that not all representations are equally well-suited to accomplish a given task, to communicate a given disciplinary concept, or to persuade a particular audience. An example will illustrate this point. Before learning about the causes of seasons, Grace's students shined their flashlights on a globe in a darkened room, noting where the rays hit directly and indirectly and inferring which parts of the globe would receive the most and least heat. Her students then represented the sun as they stood in the middle of the classroom while Grace revolved a tilted globe around them. As she walked around them, they identified which parts of the earth would be receiving the sun's direct and indirect rays.

In preparing this lesson, Grace sought the clearest way to represent the causes of seasons. Rather than explaining the causes of seasons through written language, she chose to use embodied representation, a mode that enabled the succinct communication of gradations of spatial position. In this mode, a simple body movement (stepping to a new location in the orbit) communicated a specific changing position of the earth relative to the sun. Furthermore, the flashlight enabled the students to directly observe and manipulate direct and indirect light, noting what each type of light looked like when shined on a sphere.

Just as Grace carefully selected and orchestrated representations under the belief that they would most clearly communicate disciplinary content, students, too, can select and/or produce multiple representations that best meet their purposes, justifying why they chose to communicate in a certain way. They can evaluate the clarity of their chosen representations, including the ways in which the physical features of the representation adhere (or not) to the physical features of their referents.

When Grace asked her students what was wrong with this representation, they noted that the flashlight did not accurately represent the size of the sun relative to the earth, and it did not emit a lot of light or heat. In other words, they noted the weaknesses of the representation or the ways that its features did not match the features of the sun. To further develop MRC, this conversation could have been extended as Grace asked further questions, such as If this demonstration was flawed due to the limitations of the flashlight, what is another representation we could make that would address some of these inaccuracies? What did you like about this representation? What do you think it did well?

These types of follow-up questions would further draw students into discussions regarding how and why people communicate science (or other disciplines) in particular ways, helping them develop clear frameworks for why they might make particular communicative decisions while producing their own multimodal texts.

Although Grace's students decided whether a particular representation was "apt for a particular purpose" based on the degree to which it accurately communicated features of the sun, another criterion for deciding whether a particular representation is appropriate is whether it meets the expectations of a particular audience. Milly, a language arts teacher, sought to accomplish this task when her students viewed public service announcements (PSAs) and evaluated which modes of representation (cartoons or black-and-white video, quality of music or no music, and so on) most fully enabled the advertising companies to reach targeted consumers. Whatever criterion is used, as students compare and contrast different multimodal representations and evaluate their "effectiveness" along several domains—including clarity, accuracy, persuasiveness, or appropriateness for social context—then they can develop this aspect of MRC.

(5) Describe how different representations communicate the same phenomenon in different ways and how one representation may say something that is difficult to say with another. As part of evaluating why one type of representation is more appropriate for a particular purpose than another representation, students can articulate how a given representation may "say something" that would be difficult to say through another method. This aspect of MRC is based on the premise that while any two modes may represent the same phenomenon, each mode provides a fundamentally different perspective of its referent.

Kozma and Russell (1997) initially identified this aspect of representational competence in the discipline of chemistry as they studied how experts and novices interpreted visual depictions and mathematical equations describing the same molecular bond. They argued that experts could identify when two different representations stood for the same bond, and they could explain when and why they would use a visual representation versus a mathematical one, whereas novices could not do the same. When applied to other disciplines, this principle in effect means that students can identify when multiple representations—such as visual depictions and numeric equations in mathematics—are used to represent the same phenomenon, and they can explain when to use one type of representation versus another to solve a problem or communicate a point.

Alice sought to teach her students to compare and explain different representations of the same phenomenon when they matched maps with various types of photographs before making their own multimodal "travel journals" about imaginary trips to other regions. Students viewed physical maps, as well as thematic maps where each color represented a specific range of incomes (e.g., see www.maptd.com/the-world-of-7-billion-mapping-wealth-distribution/); they viewed photographs of people in their surroundings from a range of socioeconomic backgrounds and geographic locations; they matched the photographs to the maps; and they inferred why specific photographs would correspond to specific locations on the globe based on their physical features and level of wealth.

To further solidify this aspect of representational competence, students could verbally explain why they chose particular modes in their travel journals: for instance, why they used a map to illustrate the physical features of a location instead of a photograph that could have illustrated those same features, and how the map "said something" that was difficult to say with a photograph. In all, this aspect of representational competence is based on the assumption that comparing different representations of the same phenomenon, and explaining why that particular representation was the most appropriate for what they wanted to say, supports students in becoming more proficient at disciplinary communication.

(6) Select, combine, and/or produce standard and nonstandard representations in ways that effectively communicate disciplinary concepts. Many types of representation—from maps to diagrams to graphs—have developed over time to enable people to communicate more succinctly or to accomplish tasks more effectively. Rudwick (1976), for instance, described the emergence of various visual representations in the field of geology, noting how miners developed particular types of cross sections when the need arose for them to communicate the location of mineral deposits at various depths and locations in the earth. This new type of representation enabled the miners to accomplish their work more effectively.

As in this case, new representations can enable new types of disciplinary activity or more efficiently facilitate existing activity. Because various forms of discipline-specific representation have been tested and refined over time, students can learn how to produce similar types of conventional representations in order to assist them in effectively accomplishing discipline-specific tasks. Moreover, proficiency with producing a variety of conventional representations can enable students to be recognized as potentially legitimate members within given disciplinary communities.

The ability to reproduce existing representations is not the end goal of multimodal representational competence, however. On the contrary, new forms of representation, at times spurred by new technologies, have led to innovations within each discipline. Students need not simply be inheritors of disciplinary tools that have been developed and passed down over time. Instead, students can become creators of these tools as they consider questions like How might I represent force? How might I represent the relationship between two variables? How might I represent the physical features of my community? or What types of representation would most effectively convince this particular group of people to accept my argument? These conversations draw students into the types of thinking and lines of conversation that led to the initial production of disciplinary representations (diSessa, Hammer, Sherin, & Kolpakowski, 1991; Hubber et al., 2010).

Building Literacy in Academic Disciplines through Instruction in Comprehension Strategies and MRC

In this book we address two aspects of disciplinary literacy—instruction in comprehension strategies and in multimodal representational competence—in earth science, English/language arts (ELA), mathematics, and social studies. As we elaborate in more detail in later chapters, we argue that these approaches to literacy instruction are complementary and mutually reinforcing, and that they can enrich existing instruction rather than simply being a superfluous add-on.

In the next four chapters, we describe skills recommended by discipline-specific national frameworks and standards, such as the *Next Generation Science Standards* (Achieve Inc., 2013) or the *The College, Career, and Civic Life Framework for Social Studies State Standards* (National Council for the Social Studies, 2013). We then use narratives to illustrate how middle and high school teachers helped their students to achieve those standards through literacy instruction on multiple representations. Each narrative describes one teacher's use of multimodal texts, interspersed with an analysis of how the teacher's instruction supported the students in developing MRC and strategic approaches in relation to those texts.

In addition to addressing discipline-specific national frameworks, these descriptions of literacy instruction also correspond with the Common Core State Standards (CCSS) for English/Language Arts and Literacy (National Governors Association Center for Best Practices & Council of Chief State School Officers, 2010), which emphasize that K–12 students should develop proficiency with interpreting and producing multimedia texts across several academic disciplines. In each chapter, text bars highlight the CCSS reading or writing standards that the teachers address in their instruction.

Finally, in the concluding chapter, we offer ideas on how teachers might consciously integrate a wider variety of representations into their instruction. We offer suggestions for making these representations authentic to each discipline as well as relevant to students' cultural backgrounds and interests. In sum, we assert that working with multiple representations enhances students' disciplinary understandings, and we use this book to describe how different teachers have provided literacy instruction on those representations to help their students meet national standards.

CHAPTER 2

Reading and Representing in Earth Science

Earth science addresses the interactions that occur within and across Earth's major systems—its atmosphere, biosphere, geosphere, and hydrosphere—as well as addressing the earth's attributes in relation to other planets and bodies in the universe (National Science Foundation, 2010). As students learn basic principles that undergird this branch of science, they develop understandings of the causes of many naturally occurring phenomena on earth, and they learn about how their actions affect the earth in return. Discussions of global warming, renewable versus nonrenewable resources, human acceleration of erosion, the conservation of Earth's limited supply of freshwater, and other related issues are central to helping students make informed personal decisions that protect their local and global ecosystems.

The *Next Generation Science Standards* (Achieve Inc., 2013) for this discipline emphasize that students should be able to understand and construct models in the process of learning core concepts, such as models explaining the causes of lunar phases; the causes of oceanic and atmospheric circulation; and the effects of gravity on objects within galaxies. The standards specify that these models often require multiple forms of representation. Physical models, for instance, include three-dimensional texts such as globes and embodied representations (Prain & Tytler, 2012); two-dimensional visual models include maps and diagrams; and graphical models include quantitative data displays that describe or predict patterns exhibited by physical phenomena. In other words, these standards lend themselves to a variety of visual and mathematical representations, which students can use to explain phenomena on earth.

Likewise, several of the *Next Generation Science Standards* emphasize collecting, analyzing, and interpreting data in pursuit of answers to questions. This process is likewise multimodal as students make sense of a range of information through recording a phenomenon's visual appearance, composition, temperature, and other properties. As part of collecting data from the natural world, students interpret information provided by technological equipment that measures and records physical properties, such as thermometers or visual displays from satellite systems. In addition to stressing the interpretation of nature via technological instruments, the data analysis standards also emphasize mathematical modes, such as tables that record information or graphs that synthesize information (cf. American Association for the Advancement of Science, 2009).

In earth science, the processes of interpreting data and constructing models often rely on skills associated with spatial reasoning (Kastens & Ishikawa, 2006; Orion & Ault, 2007). Indeed, questions about spatial relationships have driven major theories in this discipline, such as when Alfred Wegener became curious about the puzzle-like shape of the continents and conducted further investigations that led to his theory of continental drift, or such as when Nicolas Copernicus drew astronomical models to reason through his heliocentric theory of the universe. This reliance on spatial reasoning would suggest that spatially-oriented modes, such as physical models or images, are especially important in this discipline. Indeed, the National Research Council (2006) has affirmed the importance of spatially-oriented representations across all of the sciences when they cited Watson and Crick's seminal three-dimensional model of DNA as "exemplifying the power of a way of thinking, spatial thinking." They continued, "We suggest that spatial thinking is at the heart of many great discoveries in science" (p. 1).

Although we have underscored the importance of mathematical, visual, tactile, three-dimensional, and embodied modes in earth science, we also recognize that scientists often engage in a great deal of reading and writing in the traditional sense as they read the work of their colleagues and publish arguments of their own (Osborne, 2002). Consequently, literacy instruction in science can also teach students how to interpret and produce explanatory and argumentative writing. According to Shanahan and Shanahan (2008), scientists read these types of writing with a set of concerns that are different from readers in other disciplines. Specifically, they evaluate whether a particular article or book is scientifically credible based on the methods by which the author collected, analyzed, and reported data that aligned with a testable hypothesis and based on how the author's inferences correlated with other accepted scientific theories and suppositions. A scientist's affiliation with particular social groups can influence whether or not her work is deemed as credible (e.g., a scientist may be hired by a particular construction company to conduct research on the environmental impact of the company's building projects), but if her report leads to repeatable results it can still be regarded as meeting the standards for a quality scientific text regardless of her personal affiliations.

In accordance with national standards, students of earth science interpret and produce a wide range of modes that are embedded within larger processes of inquiry, explanation, and argumentation. The classroom examples in the following sections illustrate how earth science teachers can provide comprehension strategy instruction (CSI) and multimodal representational competence (MRC) instruction on these multimodal texts.

READING AND REPRESENTING IN THREE DIMENSIONS AND BEYOND

Typically, when we look at a representation that is printed on a page, our view of that representation is more or less fixed. That is, regardless of whether we move the paper to the right or to the left, we still see the same image, the same graph, and so on. Three-dimensional texts, however, enable us to view groups of objects from a wider range of nuanced vantage points: We can view an object's front from a diagonal angle and its back from a direct angle, we can view the spatial relationship between two objects while standing above both objects or while standing directly in front of both objects, and so forth.

Because several concepts in earth science require students to understand the changing spatial relationships between three-dimensional objects, Grace often asked her students to interpret three-dimensional texts, such as embodied representations and physical models, in addition to more traditional two-dimensional texts. The following vignette describes how Grace used a variety of three- and two-dimensional texts to teach lunar phases, followed by an analysis of how comprehension strategy instruction and MRC instruction were used to enhance students' understandings of these texts.

> A class of 6th-grade students sits in the center atrium of their middle school as Grace displays a half-yellow, half-black ball. "We're going to assume that the very end of that 7th-grade hall [points to the doorway], that parking lot, is where the sun is. So which way should I orient this ball?" After students explain that the ball should be oriented so that the yellow

FIGURE 2.1 (left). Diagram of Grace's Walk Around the Room with the Ball (= Moon), Noting Stops to Illustrate the Different Phases of the Moon

FIGURE 2.2 (right). Student's drawing of how the ball, representing the moon, appeared as Grace walked around the class while holding it.

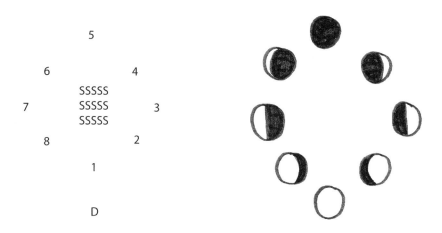

part is always facing the sun, Grace informs them that they will represent the earth and that the ball will be the moon.

Holding up the ball, she walks around her students, stopping periodically to allow students to draw what they see on the ball from their vantage point on earth (see Figure 2.1). After students had drawn several images, she asks them to predict what the ball will look like the next time she stops. By the end of Grace's orbit around "the earth," students' drawings depict a complete cycle of lunar phases (see Figure 2.2).

Grace's students return to the classroom and note how their drawings of lunar phases are similar to photographs of the moon at different phases in a lunar cycle.

In this vignette Grace assisted her students in transforming one mode into another, which is one aspect of multimodal representational competence. When Grace walked the "moon" around the "earth," her students transformed this three-dimensional representation into a series of two-dimensional images. This type of MRC instruction complements the comprehension strategy of making connections. In the case of multimodal texts, text-to-text connections can entail mapping specific sub-components of one mode to the subcomponents of another mode. In this vignette, students connected different spatial positions of a ball to individual images in a sequence. As another application of mapping sub-components of different modes onto each other, Grace could have "re-volved" around her students and stopped at a given point, asking them to identify which circle on a diagram represented her current location and to justify their response.

Another aspect of multimodal representational competence includes the ability to use features of representations to make predictions. Grace furthered the development of this aspect of MRC as she stopped at cer-tain points in the orbit and asked students to predict how the moon would appear at the next point in the orbit. In this case, students used the features of a representation (e.g., the ball's visual appearance at certain points in space and time) to make predictions about the ball's future ap-pearance. One could imagine Grace extending this type of spatial reason-ing through asking students to predict how the ball's appearance at one point would compare to its appearance at the opposite point in the orbit.

This type of instruction, in addition to building MRC, also appren-tices students to the work of scientists who seek to predict the behavior of physical phenomena based on previous observations. Furthermore, this type of instruction requires students to use the comprehension strategy of making and checking predictions, a strategy that has been shown to improve students' comprehension of printed texts.

Grace continued this lesson as described in the vignette below.

Upon returning to the classroom, Grace tells her students that they will glue their drawings of the moon on corresponding positions in the diagram in Figure 2.3. To prepare students to complete this task, she had posted a large copy of this diagram on the whiteboard with a large circle representing the sun to its right. Grace first asks her students to notice the angle from which the diagram was made: "The moon looks exactly the same in all of those pictures [points to the different phases of the moon on the diagram]. Tell me what perspective this drawing was made from. Where was the artist when he or she was drawing this? What do you think?"

"Like really high in space above it all."

"Really high in space," Grace echoes. "It's like they went to the North Pole, took off from the North Pole, flew way way way out, millions of miles away [puts finger on the circle representing earth and moves finger out as

FIGURE 2.3. Diagram on which students can paste their drawings from Figure 2.2.

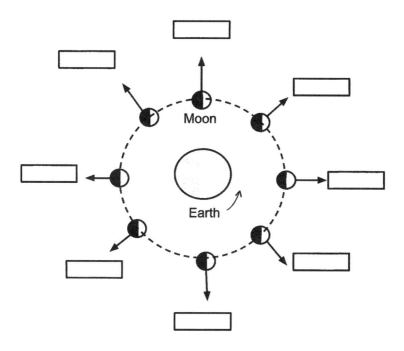

she steps away from the board], and then looked back [turns around to face the whiteboard again] and you could see the sun, and you could see the earth. This is like time lapse photography where they waited 28 days and took pictures of the moon.

"That's why the moon always looks the same, because you always have half of the moon being lit by the sun. So, they can always see from out in space, this half is lit up [points to lit half of one moon] and this one is not [points to dark half of one moon].

"Now I want you to transport yourself to earth. You're standing on earth. Take your finger or take your thumb. You see how there's this dotted line right here? [She points to the dotted line on the diagram represented in Figure 2.3.] That's the moon's orbit around earth. I want you to take your thumb, and I want you to cover up the part that's outside of the dotted line. Right here [places her finger on the outside of the dotted line over one moon in the diagram]. So if I was standing on earth, and I were to look out, I would see what is not covered. What do you see when you're looking at that?"

At this point, the students lift up their own individual diagrams so that their papers are parallel to their desks, cover the part of each circle outside of the dotted line with their fingers, and look at each circle from the position of the earth. In small groups, they discuss what they saw on each circle from the earth on the lifted paper, and they paste an image from their previous drawing of lunar phases (Figure 2.2) on each position that corresponds with what they saw.

In the latter half of her lesson Grace once again supported her students in making connections across representations: this time, between an image that was drawn from one vantage point (outer space) to an image drawn from a different vantage point (earth). She assisted students in making these connections through asking them to lift up their diagrams, which had been depicted from the vantage point of outer space, and to view them from another vantage point. From this second vantage point, students noted the similarities between the moons on the diagram from Figure 2.3 and the moons from Figure 2.2. By using the images from the previous demonstration, Grace also connected the diagram back to the original three-dimensional demonstration.

Grace not only guided her students in making these connections across representations, she also required them to explain the relationship between these representations, which is another aspect of multimodal competence. In a later lesson, students explained that the moon in the diagram appeared different from the moon in their drawingsbecause they were drawn from different spatial positions. As this vignette suggests, part of the strategy of making connections in earth science can include explaining how different representations of the same phenomena relate to one another.

In addition to making connections across three- and two-dimensional representations, students can also make inferences as they interpret these representations. Although the comprehension strategy of inferring applies to printed texts, these inferences may take different forms when applied to three-dimensional texts or images. In earth science, for example, students can make inferences about the vantage point from which a representation was made and how it would appear different from another vantage point. Grace required her students to make these types of inferences when she asked them to infer the position from which the diagram was drawn. In a second type of inference, students can conjecture how a three-dimensional object would appear from another angle. We can imagine Grace supporting this type of spatially oriented inference during the first half of the lesson as well, by asking students to imagine what the ball in her hand would look like if they were staring down at it from the ceiling. Summarizing, too, is a comprehension strategy that may take different forms as students interpret three-dimensional representations. These summaries can include syntheses of what was learned by viewing the phenomenon from multiple angles. For instance, Grace later asked her students to explain the causes of lunar phases, in effect summarizing what they had learned from the previous three- and two-dimensional texts. Students' summaries could take many forms, such as "revolving" a Styrofoam ball around a light source and explaining what was happening to it, or drawing and labeling a diagram from one vantage point and overlaying it with images from another vantage point. Because different modes exhibit different affordances, we argue that allowing students to summarize through visual and embodied means—as well as through more traditional written means—can support the clear and succinct expression of spatial concepts. Students who summarize a variety of visual, embodied, and/or written texts also gain practice with gleaning relevant information from initial sources and succinctly stating what they learned from those sources, which is a national standard for literacy in the content areas (see Textbox 2.1).

Other Applications of MRC with Three-Dimensional Texts

The principles applied in this lesson extend beyond the example of lunar phases. We offer three brief examples here as other cases illustrating how earth science teachers can encourage their students to make inferences and connections as they summarize what they have learned from a variety of three-dimensional texts and images. First, Tracy's students viewed two images of the seafloor: a direct frontal cross-section and one drawn from a slanted downward angle as though the artist were in the ocean above the seafloor. They compared and contrasted the two images, making inferences about the vantage point from which each repre-

> **TEXTBOX 2.1**
>
> **CCSS.ELA-Literacy.**
> **RST.6-8.2**
>
> Determine the central ideas or conclusions of a text; provide an accurate summary of the text distinct from prior knowledge or opinions.

sentation was drawn, before making and labeling their own clay models of the seafloor.

Second, both Grace's and Tracy's students poured heated dyed water into cold clear water, viewing the interaction from above and from the side at eye level. Then they turned to their partners and summarized their observations about the convection currents, using verbal speech and gestures.

Third, Tracy's students learned about rock formation through performing a series of actions with colored chocolate chips, such as compacting and cementing them together to form "sedimentary rocks," applying heat and pressure to them to form "metamorphic rocks," and ultimately melting and cooling them to form "igneous rocks." After students performed each action, they pointed out which photographs of rocks in their textbooks correlated with what they did to the chocolate chips.

Taken as a whole, these examples, as well as our own work in science classrooms, suggest that three-dimensional representations are especially prominent in this discipline both as a means for summarizing students' understandings (e.g., the clay model and gestures of convection) as well as a means for teaching a variety of spatial concepts. The features of these three-dimensional representations sometimes require unique reading practices, such as making inferences about how the representation would appear from multiple angles or connecting the three-dimensional representation to images on flat surfaces. Even when spatial reasoning is less prominent, as in the example of the rock cycle, students can still compare the features of three-dimensional representations to the features of other representations, as Tracy's students did when they pointed out how the visible rock particles in the chocolate chip model of the sedimentary rock compared to photographs of sedimentary rocks. In all, then, reading and representing in three dimensions include the use of many time-honored comprehension strategies such as inferring and connecting, but these strategies can be modified to fit the features and demands of these three-dimensional texts.

WHEN MATERIALITY MATTERS: INTERPRETING LABS, PHYSICAL MODELS, AND THE NATURAL WORLD

In earth science classes that we have observed, students performed actions with a wide variety of objects that represented phenomena in the physical world: They blew colored pieces of plastic across water to represent the wind's effects on the surface of the ocean; they spun globes while drawing lines down them to represent the Coriolis Effect; they placed a heat source under a clear container with dyed water to represent a hydrothermal vent, and more. At times, the physical composition of these representations was not relevant to the teachers' or students' intended messages. For instance, although Grace used a Styrofoam ball to represent the moon as she "revolved" around her students on the "earth," she could have used a plastic or rubber ball to the same effect, as long as half of the ball remained lit and half of the ball remained dark.

At other times, however, the medium actually was the message in the sense that some physically observable aspect of the representation (other than its appearance) represented some aspect of its referent, such as its temperature, viscosity, density, or rate of cooling. In other cases, teachers incorporated the natural world into their instruction. For instance, Grace brought different types of soil into her classroom so students could rub them in their hands and feel differences in the texture of clay, loam, and sand, as well as pour water over each type of soil to test how it absorbed moisture. These "texts," while not representations of items beyond themselves, enabled students to make direct observations or inferences about cause-and-effect relationships.

As this example with soil demonstrates, teachers of earth science expected their students to construct interpretations of disciplinary concepts in part through attending to the "material stuff" of the natural world and representations, and not just through noting their visual appearance as in images. We define these representations and physical phenomena as *material texts* when their texture, density, temperature, and/or other physical properties are relevant to teachers' instructional objectives. The following classroom vignettes point toward ways in which disciplinary literacy instruction—including instruction in MRC and comprehension strategies—might be reconceptualized to address students' interpretations of the physicality of various natural objects and representations.

> Groups of students in Tracy's class have placed heating lamps, representing the sun, directly over containers full of sand or water with a thermometer stuck in each of them. At 2-minute intervals, they measure the temperature of sand and water, recording it in a chart. As Tracy walks by one group of students, she notices a discrepancy between the thermometers and the

numbers in their chart. Tracy asks Tristan, a student in the group, to explain his reasoning, to which he responds that the next "longer" line above the labeled number 60 would be 65 (see Figure 2.4).

Tracy asked, "If this [points to corresponding line on thermometer] is 60, and this [points to corresponding line] is 80, what would this be [points to longer line that is in between 60 and 80]?"

"Sixty-five."

"Halfway between 60 and 80?"

"Seventy."

"So," Tracy prompted, "that means each of the little lines between [60 and 80] is going to be how many degrees?"

"Ten."

"Ten? So it's 60, 70, 80 90, 100, 110 [points to each line as she counts by 10]?"

"No."

"No, that's not going to work. If from here [points to line representing 60 degrees] to here [points to line representing 70 degrees] is 10 degrees . . . "

"Two."

"Why 2?"

After thinking for a moment, Tristan responds by pointing to each short line: "It would go 62, 64, 66, 68, 70." Tracy confirms that the short lines represent 2-degree intervals, and continues the conversation by asking how the longer lines are different from the shorter lines. Tristan says they represent 10 [-degree intervals] and points to the longer lines on the intervals as he counts by tens.

In this example sand and water became "texts" in the sense that students interpreted what happened as they were heated and cooled. Understanding the material world often requires students to use measuring instruments and technological aids, which are likewise "texts" in the sense that students make sense of what these aids are saying. In this case, Tracy sought to support Tristan's comprehension of the measuring instrument through explicitly pointing out its text features, which included labeled and unlabeled lines placed at different intervals.

To provide this instruction on text features, Tracy pointed out differences in the patterns represented by the lines: The longer, labeled lines were placed at different intervals from the shorter, unlabeled lines, and

FIGURE 2.4. Diagram of the markings on the thermometer interpreted by Tracy's students.

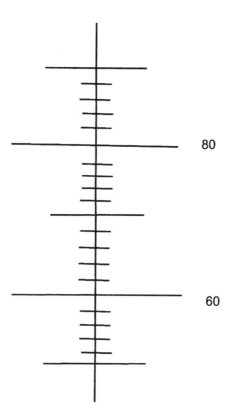

80

60

the meaning of these shorter lines was discernible in part through noticing the spacing between the longer lines. Tristan came to realize that the midlength line represented 70 degrees because it was halfway between the lines marked 80 and 60. He also realized that the shortest lines must have represented intervals of 2 degrees because there were five equally spaced intervals between 60 and 70. In this way, he used text features, such as labeled numbers and line length, to draw conclusions about the temperature of the sand.

Previous research on printed texts (Samuels & Farstrup, 2011) has suggested that attending to text features often aids students' comprehension in many ways. Through headings and subheadings, students can discern the organization of a textbook chapter, including the big "take-away" messages that the author wishes to emphasize. Moreover, text features can aid students in setting a purpose for reading when they use these features as a basis for their predictions about what will appear in the text.

Measuring instruments and material texts are obviously characterized by different features than written texts, but these features are no less important in aiding students' comprehension, as when Tristan used the features of labeled lines to draw inferences about the meanings of unlabeled lines. Ultimately, he used the features of the measuring instrument to support his conclusions about the temperature of the sand and water. This ability to interpret the features of a variety of texts and to construct inferences from them is one aspect of multimodal representational competence.

Asking questions is another comprehension strategy that includes specific applications when students interpret material texts. One common feature of material texts is that the physical activity of the user often influences what is communicated. Consequently, one specific type of question that students have to ask themselves is, "How have my physical actions influenced what I am observing?" For instance, although Tracy gave each group the same type of heating lamp, the same type of thermometer, and the same amount of sand and water, the groups recorded significantly different temperatures—some because they did not understand the features of the thermometer, some because they did not stand at eye level while reading the thermometer, and some because they put the thermometer and heating lamp in different places from other groups.

To further extend this lesson, Tracy could have displayed students' discrepant temperatures on a chart and modeled for students the types of questions that a scientist might ask when reading these discrepant temperatures: Why were Group One's temperature recordings much lower than the other groups' temperature recordings? How did Group One's lamp placement compare to the other groups' lamp placement, and how did this difference influence the heat of the sand and water? Where did this person stand when she was reading the thermometer? Thus teachers can model for students how to ask questions regarding material texts, after which they can give them opportunities to independently ask similar types of reflective questions as they manipulate and interpret a variety of material texts.

This type of questioning can be extended to written texts in science as well. Often, written claims are based on physical evidence, such as the claim that "ice shelves in Antarctica may collapse within several hundred years, given the current rate of global warming." Ice core samples are among the data collected to support this claim. However, the physical activities of the scientists influence the credibility of these claims, including the depths at which they sample the ice and whether or not they keep the ice frozen enough to bring it back to their labs to study it (Perry & McGuirk, 2013).

Consequently, the strategy of asking questions in earth science—and indeed, part of critical literacy in this discipline as a whole—entails teaching students to question how the physically observable activities of individual scientists may have influenced what the data seemed to be telling them. This type of questioning also develops students' multimodal representational competence as students learn to critically evaluate the written, numeric, and visual claims that are made in regard to material texts.

Like Tracy, Grace taught about the causes of sea and land breezes through first asking students to shine a heating lamp on water and sand as they noted the different rates of heating and cooling for both substances. The vignette below describes how Grace sought to support students' ability to produce a variety of representations in relation to the data they had collected.

"How can we record what happens to the water and sand?" she asks.

"Make a chart."

"By making a chart, exactly. What kinds of things would we need on our chart?"

"The temperature of the water and the temperature of the sand."

"Temperature of the water; temperature of the sand; anything else?"

"The time."

"And the time. So let's make a chart. On your notebook paper, let's do our time. And we're going to measure our time in what?"

"Minutes."

"Minutes. Because we're not going to do this in hours, unless you want to stay here all night long in science."

Grace begins a three-column chart on the board (see Figure 2.5) by writing the heading "Time (min)" over the first column. "Time; and then we need the temperature of the sand. Now do scientists use degrees Celsius or degrees Fahrenheit?"

"Fahrenheit," guesses one student.

"Celsius," guesses another

"Both," guesses a third.

"Celsius. That is the international system of units, or metric system," Grace says as she writes "Sand (°C)" as a header for the second column. "And we need water, also in degrees Celsius," she continues while writing "Water (°C)" as a header for a third column. "And I'm putting our units up here [points to top of each column], so I don't have to write them over and over again, although everything in those columns [runs hand down Sand and Water columns] is degrees Celsius, and everything in that first column is in minutes."

Such as Tracy explicitly taught her students about the text features of a thermometer, Grace explicitly taught her students about the text features of data charts. She modeled for students how to make these charts through labeling each heading with units of measurement that fit the students' purposes, met the standards of the scientific community, and promoted brevity of expression.

Students identified which types of information they needed to gather to help them answer their research question, which type of text would most easily and clearly enable them to record their data, and which intervals of time would be most appropriate for data collection. To further extend students' ability to produce useful representations for given purposes, Grace also could have asked students to justify their answers by arguing why they believed minutes were suitable intervals or why a chart would be ideal for recording data as opposed to other possible options.

After students record the temperature above the sand and water using the chart in Figure 2.5, Grace asks them to identify another way they could represent their table to show how the temperatures changed over time, and a student identifies a line graph. Grace agrees that this type of representation demonstrates changes over time and draws x- and y-axes on the Smartboard. Although students easily identify that the interval for the x-axis should be one minute, they begin to debate the appropriate interval for the y-axis. To help them decide, Grace asks them to identify their lowest and highest temperature, which they do.

"Very good. So we have a range of 22 to 29 degrees. Should we count by tens?"

"Fives, I think."

"So if I count by fives, I could have 0, 5, 10, 15, 20, 25, 30." For each number she says, she taps her hand on a different horizontal line on the

FIGURE 2.5. Record of the temperature of sand and water at different points in time.

Time (min)	Sand (°C)	Water (°C)
0	23	22
1	24.5	23
2	27.5	24
3	28	24
4	28	25
5	28.5	24.5
6	28.5	25
7	28.5	25.5

graph paper on the Smartboard. "So everything is going to fall between two lines [points to the line representing 20 and the line representing 30]. Are you going to be able to see a lot of changes if the graph is all between two lines?"

Several students shake their heads no or say no.

"So we want to get the smallest interval we possibly can that we can still fit everything on the graph."

"One and a half."

"We could count by one and a half," Grace agrees.

"Point five," interjects another student.

"Why should we count by halves?" she asks.

"Everything would still fit on the graph and you could see the changes in temperature."

"Yes. Probably in this instance, because we have so many half degrees," Grace says, "I would actually count by halves. But, I don't want to start at 0, .5, 1, 1.5, 2, 2.5, 3, 3.5, 4, 4.5, 5, 5.5, because that would take forever. I really want to start around 20 degrees. I can start at 20 degrees, but I need to do something so that somebody looking at this graph wouldn't go, oh you're counting by intervals of 20 and then all of the sudden start by halves. There's something I can do right here [points to where the x- and y-axes intersect]. Anybody know what I can do?"

"It's like [traces index finger in a lightning shape]."

"Yeah, it kind of looks like a little heartbeat thing [Grace traces index finger in a lightening shape]. It's a little squiggle, right? So take your pencil and go wheh, wheh, wheh, wheh, like this. [Draws lightning bolt line on the board along y-axis.] That's like you took a bunch of the graph and went chwuh, and squished it. [Grace moves both palms together like she's squishing something]. Then we can start with 20 degrees, 20 and 5 tenths, 21, 21 and 5 tenths, what would come next?" [As Grace speaks, she writes the degrees on the corresponding horizontal line on the board, moving up the y-axis.]

After assisting students in transforming observations of the physical world to recordings on a numeric table, Grace guided them in transforming a numeric table to a graph. Rather than telling students what type of representation they should make, Grace asked students to identify which representation would be best for their purposes and to justify their response. After a student had explained why he believed a line graph would be the best way to represent the data, students again identified appropriate intervals for their representation—in this case, intervals of halves for the temperature—and they justified their reasoning for selecting these intervals.

In addition to identifying appropriate intervals, students identified fitting headings for their graph, including time in x-axis and temperature in the y-axis. Finally, they also named a specific text feature (a "lightning bolt" shape) that would indicate they started their graph at 20 degrees rather than at 0 degrees. In these ways, through explicitly focusing on text features—such as headings and the inclusion of labeled intervals that fit well with the data—Grace supported her students in producing standard representations that could be recognized as legitimate within the scientific community, another component of MRC. This instruction on text features also helped students transform one set of information—the temperature of sand and water—to a chart and then to a line graph with comparable headings. In this way, she also helped students transform one mode into another, which is another component of MRC. This type of instruction also built students' proficiency with communicating quantitative information, which helped them to meet one of the national standards for literacy in science (see Textbox 2.2).

As a variation of this lesson, Grace could ask her students to work in pairs or small groups to produce a representation that compared the rate of heating and cooling for the sand and water. In this variation of the lesson, even if groups of students produced unconventional representations other than line graphs, they could compare, discuss, and evaluate the clarity of their text features, such as their headings and selection of intervals. They could identify which representations in the class most clearly communicated differences in rate of cooling and heating. This approach would also support students in developing another aspect of MRC: the production and evaluation of nonstandard representations.

> After students make a double line graph (see Figure 2.6)—with the top line representing the rate at which water heated and cooled and the bottom line representing the rate at which sand heated and cooled—they verbally summarize what they learned from viewing the slope of the line on the graphs, namely, that the sand heated and cooled more quickly, while the water heated and cooled more slowly. Finally, based on this information, they infer whether sand would be warmer or cooler than water during the day and night, and they use what they know about convection to draw arrows on the images of a beach at day and at night predicting the direction of the beach breezes at each time. They summarize the causes of sea and land breezes by writing explanations underneath their line graph and their image.

In this final component of the lesson, Grace's students used the data they had collected to make inferences about the causes of sea and land breezes. Inferences are not only a useful comprehension strategy that builds understanding a variety of visual, written, and material texts—they are also a key practice of scientists who use data to make inferences about why phenomena occur. Under guidance from Grace, students explained this phenomenon using writing, images, and their graphs, which further met the standard in Textbox 2.2. Finally, this lesson supported students'

FIGURE 2.6. Line Graphs Comparing Rate at Which Water and Sand Heat and Cool

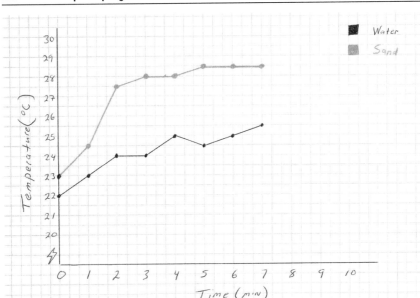

MRC as students took information that was originally expressed in a variety of modes—sand and water, tables, graphs, and images—and transformed them into verbal explanations.

The three vignettes that describe this lesson also point toward additional types of comprehension instruction that have historically been applied to printed texts but can also help students make sense of material texts. When reading printed texts, readers must often determine which information is important to the author or which information is relevant to their purpose for reading.

Similarly, when reading material texts, teachers and students can discuss which physical properties are relevant and which are not. Any material text has several features or properties—density, temperature, color, state of matter, breakability, and so forth—that may or may not be significant to a given scientific question or task. When students interpret an object's physical properties, therefore, literacy instruction can entail establishing a clear framework that focuses students' attention on significant, relevant, or important aspects of the representation, while clarifying which other physical features are not central to students' investigations.

For instance, Grace and Tracy both sought to constrain their students' interpretations of physical phenomena by instructing them to focus on one aspect of sand and water: the relative rate of change in their temperatures. This exclusive focus on rate of heating and cooling drew students' attention away from other physical features of the sand and water, such as the sand's texture or the water's density.

To further extend this lab, we imagine an explicit discussion regarding which physical features of the sand and water are significant to the outcome. Was it only the state of matter (liquid versus solid) that led to unequal heating and cooling rates? If the sand had been white instead of brown, if the sand had been finer versus coarser grained, or if the water had contained salt, would these changes have affected relative rate of heating and cooling? The comprehension strategy of determining importance of information, when applied to material texts, can include these types of explicit discussions regarding which physical features led to particular outcomes and which physical features were relatively nonessential to these outcomes.

In addition to determining the importance of information, other print-based comprehension strategies can also enhance students' scientific reasoning as they interpret a variety of material texts. One such strategy includes predicting and checking predictions. After students had discovered that the sand heated more quickly than the water, for instance, they could predict which substance would cool more quickly and justify the reasons for their predictions. Finally, at the end of the demonstration, they could revisit their predictions by speculating on why they were right, partially right, or wrong.

The comprehension strategy of inferring is also often essential to supporting students' understandings of material texts. In the discipline of science, one important type of inference is related to causation. That is, students must often infer why a particular outcome occurred as it did, justifying their inference with physical evidence. In this case, students could infer why sand heated and cooled more quickly than water. In addition to enhancing students' understandings of what happened during the demonstration, the strategies of predicting and inferring also constitute one aspect of MRC as students use features of material texts to support tentative hypotheses.

Other Applications of MRC Instruction with Material Texts

The sand/water demonstration provided an example of how two teachers supported students' MRC regarding material texts, but the sciences abound with many other examples of material texts as students interpret the causes and effects of physical phenomena. In this lesson, the sand and the water in the containers were a proxy for the sand and water on the beach, but in other cases the relationship between the representation and its referent were less connected. In one lesson, for example, Grace used a chocolate-covered cherry to represent the layers of the earth. Students cut the cherry, noting each layer's state of matter, its relative thickness, and its viscosity. They compared these attributes to the visual and written depictions of the layers of the earth in their textbooks, then verbally articulated to a partner what they noticed about the similarities and differences between the layers of the cherry and the layers of the earth.

In this example Grace helped her students distinguish relevant or targeted physical attributes from the irrelevant or untargeted physical attributes by setting a clear framework for "reading" the chocolate-covered cherry: Students were to look for the physical properties of relative thickness, viscosity, and state of matter, but not for other physical properties such as color, relative density, or temperature. She provided other representations, such as the textbook diagrams, with the intention of constraining students' interpretations of the cherry (cf. Ainsworth, 2006), and students also explicitly articulated how the representation was both *like* the earth as well as *unlike* it.

As suggested by this example, it is not always possible for teachers to provide students with direct experience with the physical world (e.g., by observing layers of the earth), so they often use representations whose physical features mimic the features of their referents in some way. These material representations bring their own sets of challenges: Students may focus on an aspect of the representation that is not meant to represent its referent (e.g., they may assume that the center of the earth is soft and porous, like the cherry), and they may not draw scientifically acceptable conclusions about the target phenomenon based on the limitations of the representation.

To assist students in distinguishing relevant or focal aspects of the representation, therefore, teachers can ask students to verbally explain the relationship between material texts and what they represent, followed by further discussions to prevent misunderstandings. This type of instruction meets national standards for literacy in science, such as the standard in Textbox 2.3, because it requires students to compare and contrast information learned from a material text to information learned from a written text. Moreover, this type of instruction highlights the limitations of representations, such as when Grace's students noted that the layers of the chocolate-covered cherry were not proportionally scaled to the layers of the earth. They remarked that, although the chocolate layer was thin compared to the other layers, it was not as thin as the crust of the earth would be if a scaled representation of the earth was the size of a chocolate-covered cherry. This type of explicit discussion on the weaknesses of representations also helped students to meet another national standard for literacy in science (see Textbox 2.4), as they evaluated the disadvantages of this particular representation.

In sum, material texts such as those described above are often central to the work of science. Literacy instruction on these texts can include explicitly addressing their focal versus nonfocal features, questioning how physical actions influenced the text's material properties, teaching students how their observations can be transformed to a variety of graphs and charts, and modeling how to use representations to draw connections to or inferences about the material world.

MULTIMODAL REPRESENTATIONAL COMPETENCE AND SCIENTIFIC ARGUMENTATION

Although we assert that a variety of three-dimensional and material texts are central to earth science, we do not mean to imply that printed texts should play a minor role in literacy instruction in this discipline. On the contrary, Osborne (2002) has argued that science without instruction in print-based literacy is like a "ship without a sail" because verbal or written language often frames students' understanding of other modes. Furthermore, several researchers (Kuhn, 2010; Newton, Driver, & Osborne,

1999) have emphasized that students should be able to construct written scientific arguments using empirically valid claims. We use the following vignette as a springboard to discuss ways in which MRC can also work in conjunction with instruction in written scientific argumentation to support students' literacy in earth science.

> After learning about the characteristics of rocks, Tracy's students participate in a computer simulation. Their job is to help clients who want to accomplish a variety of tasks, such as building a monument in a rainy and polluted area or scrubbing callouses from their skin. These hypothetical clients need advice on which rocks should be used for each task. To help these clients, each student selects from among a handful of rocks by clicking on that rock on a computer screen. Each student then watches what happens during the computer simulation when the rock is used for that task.
>
> When a student chooses to build a monument out of granite, for instance, it withstands acid rain and tourist wear and tear, as opposed to a monument built from sandstone. However, the monument made out of sandstone is easier to cut and cheaper to replace. After observing the outcomes associated with various rocks, the students write a letter in which they advise clients to select a particular rock for their task, citing specific characteristics of the rock that make it appropriate for selection. Tracy invites students with different answers to share their letters and argue on behalf of their rock selection.

In addition to emphasizing national standards related to argumentation during this lesson (e.g., Textbox 2.5), Tracy also addressed cross-cutting STEM (science, technology, engineering, and mathematics) concepts (National Research Council, 2011). Specifically, this activity introduced engineering thinking, such as considering trade-offs when designing a product. In this case, when students selected material for the monument, they had to decide whether longevity was more important than ease of cutting, or vice versa.

> **TEXTBOX 2.5**
>
> **CCSS.ELA-Literacy. WHST.6-8.1**
>
> Write arguments focused on discipline-specific content.

An extension of this lesson could take into consideration that engineers' and scientists' recommendations/findings are often multi-representational. Thus Tracy's students could produce and evaluate multi-representational letters, including screenshots of line graphs that represent the rate at which the two rocks weathered or photographs that depict the corrosive effects of acid rain on sandstone and granite after a certain amount of time. In addition to evaluating the overall effectiveness of the written argument, students could also discuss which multi-representational letter made the strongest case in terms of its potential to persuade the client. This ability to use multiple representations to persuade others is another component of MRC and scientific literacy that can be built with practice.

Critical Literacy in Earth Science

This component of MRC is related to critical literacy in earth science, which includes the ability to critique scientific representations and the larger arguments in which they are embedded, despite the seemingly authoritative nature of these arguments. Scholars (Bazerman, 1998; Halliday & Martin, 1993) have noted that scientific language is often presented as beyond the realm of human opinion or fallibility, often omitting markers that would indicate a degree of subjectivity, such as *in my opinion* or *I believe that*.

Regardless of the often disinterested presentation of earth science, however, this discipline has long been fraught with disagreement among competing human actors who seek funding and support from powerful organizations (Latour, 1987; Knain, 2001). From Nicolas Copernicus, whose argument against a geocentric universe was seen as a direct challenge to Catholicism in the 16th century, to modern-day politicians backed by oil companies, who argue against the existence of global warming, arguments in earth science have long been made in the context of larger societal trends. Critical literacy in this discipline therefore includes looking beyond the seemingly objective nature of claims as students learn to question the position of the author.

These markers of objectivity extend beyond scientific language. Many scientific images likewise do not include features that overtly indicate an individual's shaping influence on the image, such as the artist's signature or personal style. Consequently, just as students can learn to question the validity of written claims, they can likewise question other representations, such as images and graphs that are used to make seemingly objective claims as well. Grace sought to develop this type of critical literacy in her students when she asked them to read materials warning against the dangers of dihydrogen monoxide on a website (dhmo.org). This website included photographs of eroded areas that had been contaminated with DHMO, as well as a logo from the United States Environmental Assessment Center. After all students had agreed to sign a petition banning the substance, Grace revealed that DHMO was an unusual name for water and cautioned students against accepting advice just because scientific language and photographs made them appear legitimate. We can imagine critical discussions of other scientific representations as well, such as comparing two line graphs depicting the same physical phenomenon—one with larger intervals and one with smaller intervals—to show that the one with smaller intervals may make the changes appear more pronounced to those who do not read the intervals carefully.

In this section, we envision scientific argumentation as being multimodal; that is, students can produce written arguments that include multiple forms of representation in the service of proving a point. Moreover, they can also learn to critique the arguments that others make through a variety of representations, such as line graphs, diagrams, and photographs. Because many everyday texts—such as health information or advertisements—use so-called scientific representations and evidence to support their claims, students who learn to ask critical questions of these texts can be better equipped to evaluate them in the process of making informed decisions.

SUPPORTING MULTIMODAL SCIENCE LITERACY THROUGH THINK-ALOUDS

Students can be apprenticed into reading by explicitly learning how skilled readers approach texts and by having multiple opportunities to practice similar approaches themselves (Schoenbach, Greenleaf, & Murphy, 2012). This task is often accomplished in part through think-alouds as skilled readers model their thought processes for novices while reading a disciplinary text. In effect, the rationale behind think-alouds is to make invisible thought processes visible to students so that they can practice using similar thought processes.

In traditional think-alouds on printed texts teachers usually project an excerpt from a text on a Smartboard and annotate it as they think aloud about the text through asking clarification questions, making inferences, and verbally articulating other comprehension strategies. As part of the process of a think-aloud, teachers also evaluate texts according to discipline-specific concerns: In the case of science, for instance, the teacher could read a lab report and evaluate the methods by which the lab was conducted.

Students then have opportunities to practice using these approaches to reading themselves, either verbally (through articulating what they are thinking to peers), or on paper (through writing their connections, clarifying questions, and visuals in the margins of a text). Ideally, teachers would provide these opportunities for multiple texts over a significant duration of time so students could get repeated practice with "thinking like a reader" as well as "thinking like a scientist."

We argue that, much as novice students can develop cognitive frameworks for approaching printed texts, so, too, they can develop cognitive frameworks for approaching three-dimensional demonstrations and material representations. In other words, the rationale behind think-alouds for printed texts likewise applies to a variety of multimodal texts. Imagine, for example, Grace modeling what she thought as she interpreted the lunar phases demonstration, through making comments such as these:

- I wonder what the ball would look like if I were standing on the roof of our school, looking down at it?
- I am predicting that, because the moon looks like a half circle at this point in the orbit, it will look like a half circle, with the other half lit, at the opposite point in the orbit. Oh, look, my prediction was right.
- I have a question: How is this representation scaled according to time? When it takes me a few seconds to complete one-eighth of the orbit, how long would that take the moon in "real" time? How long would the whole orbit around the earth take?

Similarly, when interpreting a natural phenomenon, science teachers can model what a scientist would think while interpreting the same phenomenon, including making inferences about causation, noting when their predictions about the behavior of the phenomenon were wrong, asking questions about how a scientist's physical actions influenced outcomes, and so forth.

Students can likewise conduct verbal or written think-alouds on a variety of three-dimensional, material, and visual texts, at times with prompts to guide their thinking, such as the following:

- I predict that . . . because . . .
- My prediction was . . . [right/wrong/partially right]. What actually happened was . . . because . . .
- I infer that . . . was caused by . . . because . . .
- If viewed from another perspective, I think . . . would look like . . . .
- [This representation] is like [referent] in these ways . . . .
- [This representation] is unlike [referent] in these ways . . .
- When I performed this action . . . I noticed . . . [e.g., when I hit the water/cornstarch mixture hard, I noticed it acted like a solid] . . .
- I still have questions about . . .

Thus, just as students can gain a greater understanding of scientific concepts through becoming more strategic, purposeful, and practiced readers of print texts (Greenleaf et al., 2011), so too can students gain deeper understandings of scientific concepts from becoming more strategic, purposeful, and practiced at interpreting a variety of non-print texts as well.

CHAPTER INSIGHTS

Students of earth science often interpret texts with discipline-specific characteristics, such as three-dimensional models or texts whose physical properties are relevant to disciplinary concepts. Throughout this chapter, we argued that comprehension strategy instruction is relevant for these texts as well for printed texts, although CSI may be modified to account for their unique features. For instance, the strategy of *making connections* may entail mapping the visual features of one mode onto another; the strategy of *inferring* may include conjecturing what a representation looks like when cross-sectioned or viewed from a different angle; the strategy of *determining relevant information* may include discussing which physical features led to particular outcomes; and the strategy of *summarizing* may include using spatially-oriented modes, such as embodied representations and three-dimensional models, to explain phenomena.

These comprehension strategies link to the development of multi-modal representational competence. As students compare and contrast the information presented in multiple representations, as they transform one representation into another, and as they evaluate the limitations of their representations, they become more proficient at scientific communication and reasoning (Hubber, Tytler & Haslam, 2010; Kozma & Russell, 1997). Moreover, critiquing multiple representations fosters critical scientific literacy as students learn to question the claims presented in graphs, data charts, photographs, and other modes as well as the claims presented in writing. Ultimately, we assert that literacy instruction with and on multiple representations helps students to meet national standards as they develop enriched understandings of disciplinary concepts.

CHAPTER 3

Reading and Representing in English/Language Arts

In large part, the discipline of English has been dedicated to the study and production of texts. How texts are structured at a micro- or macro-level; how features contribute to a text's overall meaning or aesthetic value; how texts are shaped and used for different purposes in different contexts; and strategies for communicating are all part of the designated province of this discipline according to state and national standards (e.g., National Governors Association Center for Best Practices & Council of Chief State School Officers, 2010). If this discipline is largely focused on the interpretation and production of texts, then what is a text in English/language arts?

The National Council of Teachers of English (NCTE & International Reading Association, 1996) moved toward answering this question when they specified in the first line of their national standards that "students read a wide range of print and non-print texts" (p. 3), including texts produced for informational and aesthetic purposes. This statement recognizes that much of communication in contemporary society is profoundly multimodal, integrating features such as layout, color, font size, images, music, and verbal speech (Kress, 2003). Therefore, students who wish to be informed, critical, and empowered consumers and participants in digital settings must "apply knowledge of . . . media techniques . . . to create, critique, and discuss print and non-print texts" (NCTE/IRA, p. 3).

Media techniques include techniques that are shared with printed texts, such as the use of particular phrases to connote meanings, but they extend beyond these techniques as well. For instance, advertisers often use the timbre of people's voices—whether deep and husky, childlike, or somewhere in between—to connote a particular tone or mood (van Leeuwen, 1999), and web designers use spatial layout and relative size on a page to emphasize some elements of their message while minimizing others (Kress & van Leeuwen, 2006). In accordance with the Common Core State Standards' emphasis on analyzing craft and structure, students can begin to recognize how these specific sub-components of multimodal texts contribute to an overall tone, theme, or meaning.

Indeed, the CCSS, like other national language arts standards, underscore that students should be able to analyze "information presented in diverse media and formats" (CCSS.ELA-Literacy.SL.8.2). As they analyze this information, they should be able to cite textual evidence to explain the inferences they drew (CCSS.ELA-Literacy.RL.8.1). Although teachers commonly ask students to cite textual evidence as they read literary and informational print texts, this practice applies to multimodal texts as well. When definitions of texts are expanded to include multiple modes, citing textual evidence may include pointing out how a crescendo in music correlated with a particular spoken phrase for dramatic effect, or noting how web designers used particular color schemes to convey their attitudes toward their subjects.

According to the CCSS, in addition to interpreting multimodal texts, students should also have opportunities to communicate using "multimedia and visual displays," especially those that are produced using technology (CCSS. ELA-Literacy.SL.8.5; CCSS.ELA-Literacy.W.8.6). After students have analyzed how other authors use multimodal means to craft an argument or tell a story, they can then try similar techniques in their own multimodal productions. In a digital age, "developing a topic with well-chosen facts" can include selecting pertinent photographs and graphs that add credibility to the student's claims (CCSS.ELA-Literacy.W.8.2). Much as students evaluate and revise their own print-based writing, they can evaluate the effectiveness of their multimodal narratives or informational texts. In the latter case, in addition to revising for word choice or organizational structure of the writing, they can determine the "advantages and disadvantages of using different mediums to present a particular topic" (CCSS. ELA-Literacy.RI.8.6). In other words, they can identify how the modes they selected held particular affordances as opposed to other modes.

Of course, although digital technologies are becoming omnipresent in many adolescents' lives, countless valued texts in this discipline are not digital. Through discussions around classic novels, contemporary graphic novels, or young adult literature, students of this discipline are invited to speculate on characters' psychological states and motivations, to empathize with their dilemmas, to evaluate the morality of their actions, and to reflect on the implications for their own personal lives (Lee & Spratley,

2010). One method for building empathetic understandings of literature is through drama or embodied representation, a practice which has a long tradition in English/language arts (Applebee, 1974; Graff, 1987). Embodying characters can help students to "*be* the book" (Wilhelm, 1997) and get "*into* the story" (Miller & Saxton, 2004) as they try to act and speak as a character would (Franks, Durran, & Burn, 2008; Schneider, Crumpler, & Rogers, 2006). In other words, embodied representations can help students meet the disciplinary goal of connecting on a personal level to the complexity of characters' dilemmas.

In sum, English as a discipline has a long history of focusing on the medium through which human beings communicate with each other and with themselves: language. The National Council of Teachers of English has expanded this definition of language to include "visual language" such as images and other forms of representation that are popular on digital platforms. As students read for entertainment, write for personal expression, argue a point, or participate in a host of other communicative tasks, English as a discipline can enable students to reflect on the power and forms of texts as they communicate for different purposes in online and offline settings.

IMAGE, MUSIC, SPEECH, WRITING: PRODUCING DIGITAL NARRATIVES IN ENGLISH/LANGUAGE ARTS

Kathryn, a middle school language arts teacher whose students had recently immigrated from Mexico or Somalia, believed that literacy encompassed the ability to interpret and produce a wide array of visual and digital texts as well as more traditional printed texts. She integrated multiple forms of media in a unit whose central questions addressed how geographical backgrounds, familial traits and traditions, personal characteristics, values, life experiences, and other factors worked together to produce identity. As part of this unit, her students noted how image-makers used particular techniques to communicate aspects of their subjects' identity. As a culminating project, students produced a multimodal digital narrative, which included several written, visual, and aural components. The following vignette illustrates how Kathryn, drawing from Kress and van Leeuwen's (2006) "grammar of images," began a discussion on analyzing and producing images.

Kathryn's students work in small groups, each of which has a stack of about 20 self-portraits from contemporary and historical artists from all over the world, ranging from Frida Kahlo to Aaron Douglas. The students place the cards into piles based on the different characteristics they notice in the images. One group mentions the realism of images, noting that some self-portraits depict the artist as he or she would appear in a photograph, but other images look altered, such as a self-portrait of a man with a neon yellow waxy face. Another group notes that several of the images depict people doing something such as pushing against a wall or painting, whereas other self-portraits depict people who are sitting still. One student notices that a few of the artists seem to be looking directly at him, but the other artists are not. Yet another group notices that in some pictures, only the artist's face is visible, whereas in others the viewer can see the whole body.

Kathryn introduces her students to the formal terminology surrounding these features and asks students why different artists might use them. For instance, image-makers engage in *framing* when they decide whether to portray some subjects more closely (e.g., the viewer can see only faces) or more distantly (e.g., the viewers can see people's whole bodies with space around them). Image-makers also select a level of *modality,* which refers to the degree of objectivity and realism assumed in the image. Students point out that the man with the waxy yellow face looks unrealistic and comedic (indicating a low modality), whereas some self-portraits are faithful to what artists would see if they looked in a mirror (high modality). People who pose for the viewers while making *eye contact* enter into a direct relationship with their viewers, whereas those who continue in daily activity without acknowledging the viewers' presence do not offer the same kind of relationship.

Using these terms, Kathryn questions why some artists portray themselves as being closer and others portray themselves as farther away; why some paintings look more like a cartoon and others look more like a photograph; why some artists look directly at the viewer and others seem to continue on their daily activities; and so forth. When students ask further questions about these terms, Kathryn demonstrates what she means by taking photographs of a student volunteer using different techniques. For instance, Nadia looks directly at the camera while Kathryn shoots her photograph from eye level; she sits looking downward as Kathryn positions herself above her to take a photograph; and she gazes into space as Kathryn positions herself below her and takes the photograph from an angle that looks up at her. Kathryn immediately places the photographs on the interactive whiteboard for a group analysis, in which students use the introduced terms to describe the effects of the techniques in the photographs. They note, for instance, that the absence of eye contact seemed to signal detachment from the viewer, while looking up at Nadia made her seem more powerful.

Students subsequently create images of themselves, which serve as the introduction of their digital narratives. In writing, they explain why they chose to craft their images as they did, using the specific terminology that they had learned. Nadia, for example, adds white light around her body in a photograph of herself, reminiscent of a halo. She explains that she intended for her smile, close framing, direct frontal angle, and eye contact with the audience to invite people into a welcoming relationship with her, while the white light and soft colors further represent warmth and gentleness. Nadia wants to be a teacher and frames her photograph beside a chalkboard, while the images in other students' narratives include other types of poses, framing, angles, lighting, and background objects. Another student, Antonio, for instance, darkens his photo and looks away from the viewer in order to seem mysterious because "I want them [my viewers] to wonder who I am."

This example highlights methods by which English/language arts teachers can assist their students in developing aspects of multimodal representational competence (see "Multimodal Representational Competence Across Disciplines" in Chapter 1). Students "used specific features of representations to support inferences or claims"—in this case, they used features of self-portraits to support claims about the artists' identities and values. Students further "described how different representations communicated the same phenomenon in different ways," another aspect of MRC, as they identified how an image of the same person communicated a different tone or meaning depending on the angle at which it was taken, its modality, or its color scheme. This activity also reinforced another aspect of MRC—producing texts that effectively communicate disciplinary themes—as students generated and explained self-portraits that communicated aspects of their own identities using the same general techniques as the professional models.

In addition to furthering students' MRC, Kathryn also increased her students' comprehension through teaching them how to apply the comprehension strategy of inferring. In some ways, making inferences about visual texts is similar to making inferences about written texts. In the case of both images and writing, students can make inferences with respect to the *content* of the work. For instance, based on the jewelry, rich curtains, pillar, and balcony in Frida Kahlo's *Time Flies,* students inferred that Kahlo intended to depict her subject as being wealthy. As with writing, students can also make inferences about how the *form* of the work contributes to its overall meaning, with one difference: Whereas form in writing includes aspects such as rhyme, scheme, meter, syntax, and other comparable techniques, form in images includes framing, angle, spatial placement, body position, and color. Making inferences about images therefore requires using a different type of "form" as the basis for inferences.

Accordingly, Kathryn's students discussed how images' features contributed to their overall message. First, they made inferences regarding the presumed social distance between the viewer and the subject of the image through noting each image's framing. According to Hall (1964; cf. Kress & van Leeuwen, 2006), the concept of *framing* stems from the degree of physical proximity that people have with those around them. When one person is an arm's distance away from another, or close enough for a handshake, then in many cultures the two people are at a friendly yet professional distance. When this principle is applied to images, subjects that are framed with a visible torso and face—or what would be seen from about an arm's length away—are considered to have a close social relationship to the viewer, whereas images that are framed more closely indicate a more intimate relationship between the subject of the image and the viewer, and images that are framed from farther away communicate a more removed and distant relationship.

Second, they made inferences regarding the power relationship between the viewer and the subject of the image. As Nadia explained, she used close framing in her self-portrait with the intention of encouraging viewers to feel close to her. To further accomplish this goal, Nadia also made eye contact with the viewer, a technique that invites viewers into a direct relationship, unlike images that depict people engaged in activity without acknowledgment or awareness of the viewer's presence. The *angle* at which the photograph is taken is another method by which image-makers establish particular kinds of relationships with the viewer. When an image is taken from a direct frontal angle, the viewer literally sees eye to eye with the subject who is placed at an equal height to the viewer, as opposed to when the viewer looks up to or down upon a subject. Media analysts (e.g., Monaco, 1981) have long noted that the downward angle has been used to foster feelings of condescension or pity toward the subject of the image, whereas the upward angle is intended to foster feelings of awe or a sense of the subject's power. Kathryn's students made inferences about the effects of angle placement when they noted how Nadia appeared different when photographed from above, below, and at eye level.

Finally, in addition to making inferences about power and social distance, viewers can also make inferences in regard to the tone of images, or the image-makers' attitude toward their subjects. One indicator of tone is color. To be sure, colors do not have universal meanings, but instead have uses that vary according to time period, location, and social group. Despite societies' variance in use of color, students can identify how they have seen similar colors and make inferences about why image-makers selected particular color schemes to communicate tone. Nadia engaged in this type of reasoning when she inferred that white, soft lights would communicate warmth, while Patricio inferred that a darkened photo would communicate a sense of mystery. Thus, students can conduct close readings of images much as they conduct close readings of written work: by noting specific subcomponents and inferring how they contribute to an overall tone, theme, or effect (see Textbox 3.1).

> **TEXTBOX 3.1**
>
> **CCSS.ELA-Literacy.RL.8.1**
>
> Cite the textual evidence that most strongly supports an analysis of what the text says explicitly as well as inferences drawn from the text.

Students used their self-portraits to introduce their digital narratives, but Kathryn's literacy instruction did not stop at explicit instruction on images. She also wanted her students to become more proficient creators of a variety of written and aural texts. The following vignette describes how she assisted her students in developing multimodal competence that extended beyond the interpretation and production of images.

Students read the children's story *An Angel for Solomon Singer* (Rylant, 1992), after which Kathryn asks them to use evidence from the story to identify Solomon's characteristics. One student argues that a major characteristic of Solomon is that he is lonely because he always eats at the restaurant by himself and the illustrations of his life are gray. After Kathryn generates a list of his characteristics on the whiteboard, students write a biopoem as though they were Solomon. They later use this biopoem as a model for their own biopoems; likewise, they use models of other high school students' "I Am From" poems as mentor texts for their own (Christensen, 2000).

After reading additional model narratives, students write about a significant event from their own lives and revise each narrative based on peer and teacher comments. After reading their poems and narratives aloud and obtaining feedback from their peers, students then select which poems and narrative excerpts they want to read aloud in their final digital products.

Upon finishing their written work, students now turn to selecting additional images and music to accompany their verbal speech. Using the principles from the image analysis activity, such as the fact that image-makers consciously select particular objects or locations to communicate identity, they search for public domain images and music that fit the tone or content of their narratives. They produce storyboards that show how each mode works together for different frames in their narrative, and they use Photostory 3 to combine the different modes into a coherent work. These digital stories are later uploaded into podcasts.

As an "after-writing activity," Kathryn meets individually with students and listens to them explain why they selected particular music, images, and pieces of writing to communicate a particular message or tone. In this individual meeting, Misael explains why he chose to introduce the story of his cousin's death with a photograph of a weathered statue whose rain-soaked face made her appear as though she were weeping. Although statues are not a part of his story, he says he wants to set a tone that shows his sense of sadness.

Patricio, by contrast, wants his podcast to portray him as tough, and consequently he selects photographs of National Football League players being tackled, as well as a Bad Boys II movie poster of Martin Lawrence and Will Smith walking away from burning cars. This latter image accompanies the verbally read line from his poem: "I am from popcorn, fighting movies, and Coca-Cola." Consistent with this focus, he says he wants to use rap music as his background. Nadia, by contrast, chooses high-toned, fast-paced, airy bell music as well as bright colors and cartoons for her podcast. She asserts that these elements work together to express her happiness. Although each podcast is different, students demonstrate that they purposefully select images, music, and writing because they work together to portray their character traits or "things that are important to me."

In this example Kathryn supported her students in developing MRC as they "selected, combined, and produced representations to effectively communicate disciplinary concepts" such as the concept of *identity.* Although using other people's work (e.g., images) has historically been considered plagiarism in schools, the ability to choose, juxtapose, and/or modify existing representations in the digital age has been recognized as a distinct form of literacy in its own right (Knobel & Lankshear, 2008), and Kathryn helped her students accomplish this task conscientiously and ethically by accessing public domain works and by articulating the reasons behind each selection. Her students also explained why their selected representations were more appropriate for their purpose than other representations, which is another aspect of MRC, as when Nadia said that she chose bright cartoons to convey happiness as opposed to the gray, rainy photographs selected by Misael.

These aspects of MRC can be supported through the comprehension strategy of making connections, as students justify their selection of particular modes by making connections to how they have seen or heard that mode being used in the past. Any mode—whether body movements, images, clothes, writing, or music—has a *provenance,* which includes the previous societal contexts in which that mode has appeared (Kress & van Leeuwen, 2001). For instance, image-makers can choose to tell their stories through black-and-white photographs, cartoonlike characters, impressionistic drawings, and so forth. Because many comics have portrayed characters whose purpose is to entertain or to make an audience laugh, the decision to portray exaggerated characters through cartoons can reflect this provenance, as when Nadia used cartoons to reflect a lighthearted and happy tone. Conversely, black-and-white photographs—common to historical documentaries—were used before new technologies enabled color photography. The use of black-and-white photography also can reflect a more sober provenance, as when Misael chose a primarily gray image to reflect his sense of loss and sadness over his cousin's death.

Consequently, one method by which English teachers can support students in making connections is by helping them identify other contexts in which they have seen or heard particular types of clothes, images, or music that are similar to the modes they are viewing. Questions such as "What does this (song/image/item of clothing) remind you of? Where else have you seen this type of (image/music) used? What are its geographical or historical origins?" can help students understand why text-makers choose particular forms of music, images, and body movements.

Kathryn's students engaged in this kind of analysis as they explained their selection of images and music in their digital narratives. Carlos, for example, wanted mariachi music to accompany his verbal narrative because "It is from Mexico, and I am from Mexico." Another student explained that she selected images of buildings whose architecture reminded her of plazas in her home state and country. One aspect of making connections in regard to multimodal texts can include inferring how the provenance of each mode influences the overall message of the work, including what the author implies about her or his identity through depicting architecture, clothing, music, and images that are reminiscent of particular geographic regions, classes, time periods, or social groups. This strategy of making connections helps students engage in MRC as they justify why they used particular kinds of modes based on how they have seen those modes used in the past, as when Patricio assumed that rap could convey a "bad boy" personality based on how he had heard rap used in the past.

Other Applications of MRC with Digital Narratives

In the example above, students selected from a large variety of images and music to communicate aspects of their identities. Other platforms for producing multimodal digital texts impose more constraints on representation by requiring students to choose among a more limited set of predetermined options. One such website is GoAnimate (www. goanimate.com), which allows students to select among available avatars, background settings, objects, movements, and international accents to produce an animated story in which characters interact with each other.

John's ELA students used this platform to produce stories in which literary characters interacted with each other in ways that were consistent with their traits and behaviors. As with Kathryn, John's students justified why they made the representational choices they did in relation to their characters: why they chose particular accents, types of music, clothes, words, or background settings to portray aspects of each character's traits. One student explained why he chose clothes that made the character appear to be an affluent adult professional, for instance, when he could have selected other available clothes on the website whose provenance suggested they belonged to characters from different age groups, classes, time periods, and occupations.

Regardless of whether students make their own representations, choose among available representations on the Internet, or use a platform with a predetermined set of representations to tell a story—MRC can be developed in part as English students justify the connotations of the modes they chose based on their features, based on how they have seen these modes used in the past, and based on the tone, theme, or character traits they wish to communicate. We imagine that these conversations about representation may even take the form of discussing which digital platform is best for the particular story students want to tell. Perhaps some stories would be best told through platforms with playful animal cartoon characters (e.g., Make Beliefs Comix at www.makebeliefscomix. com), whereas other stories would be more powerful if students could read them in their own voices using their own photographs. In other words, discussions about which modes are best can extend to discussions about which digital platforms would most easily allow students to generate those modes. This type of instruction also meets national standards that require students to reflect on which mediums would be best for communicating their particular ideas (see Textbox 3.2).

> **TEXTBOX 3.2**
>
> **CCSS.ELA.RI.8.7**
>
> Evaluate the advantages and disadvantages of using different mediums (e.g., print or digital text, video, multimedia) to present a particular topic or idea.

EMBODIED REPRESENTATION IN ENGLISH/LANGUAGE ARTS

Digital platforms—although central to contemporary life for many people—are not the only compelling media for persuasion and expression. On the contrary, a variety of printed, three-dimensional, and embodied representations are also powerful venues for self-expression. In addition to focusing on the written word, English/language arts has a long tradition of being tied to one particular medium: theatre (Applebee, 1974). This type of representation combines several modes: written language (e.g., reading play scripts), verbal speech (e.g., articulating clearly and using inflection or tone to communicate meaning), clothing and interior design (e.g., choosing items that reflect particular social contexts), and, of course, embodiment (e.g., choosing postures and body movements to indicate the actions and emotions of particular characters). Due to the particularly personal nature of theatre—where even one's breath can "mean" something about a character—many scholars have argued that theatre is especially suited to engender a deep empathy for historical and contemporary people and/or for fictional characters.

Shirley often sought to incorporate embodied representation into her instruction under the belief that it engaged her students and connected them to literature at a more intimate level. The following vignette describes how Shirley modified existing lesson ideas (Buehl, 2009; Smagorinsky & O'Donnell-Allen, 1998) by adding embodied representations to support students' understanding of the young adult novel *Maniac Magee* (Spinelli, 1990).

> Shirley distributes strips of paper to her students, each of which contains a carefully selected quote by a main character in the novel. One pair of students, for instance, analyzes the quote, "Yo—fishbelly! . . . Maybe nobody told you—I'm badder than ever. I'm getting badder every day. I'm almost afraid to wake up in the morning 'cause-a how bad I mighta got overnight." They write down a list of characteristics that they infer this character (Mars Bar) exhibits as evidenced by the quote, including being a trash-talker, a show-off, and a kid on the streets, as well as having a sense of humor.
>
> Shirley asks students to share their quotes and their written lists, and she compiles them all on the whiteboard on a chart with a column for each character. Shirley's students then choose a character and enact several physical poses that they feel would most fully represent the stated attributes of their selected character, such as a repeated "gangsta" hand movement, cocked head, and half smile for Mars Bar, and a hand on the hip and a wagging, pointing finger for Amanda Beale, another character who scolds her younger siblings.
>
> Still in character, students walk around the room and interact with other characters,while maintaining physical postures and verbal speech that indicate their defining traits. Some students represent more dominant, aggressive characters through gestures such as balled fists, while another student represents a more passive, elderly character through hunching over, putting his head downwards, and shuffling with his hands in his pockets. Other people in the class guess who each character is based on the poses that they struck. Afterward, they comment on whether individual classmates stayed true to the story through his or her poses.
>
> In another lesson, Shirley tells students they will make a "body biography," or a life-size outline of a body that represents the core personality traits and actions of a character from the novel. Students populate the body outline with symbols, images, and quotations that they feel are most illustrative of their selected character. Before outlining the

body, Shirley asks students to think about the pose that would define the character and use that pose as the backdrop of the body biography.

Students work individually to create their body biographies, which they present to their small groups. They explain why they chose the pose, images, symbols, and quotations they did. One student, for example, explains he drew Maniac in a running pose as his defining characteristic, with an image of a band-aid on a scar representing his healing from his parents' death and with two pairs of sneakers beside each other to symbolize Mars Bar and Maniac's friendship. Another draws Mars Bar flexing his bicep in a show-off posture, outlining his skin in barbed wire but placing a marshmallow for his heart, explaining that he was tough on the outside but inside he cared for Maniac. Another depicts Grayson as lying down to represent that he was old, tired, and close to the time of his death, with gray items inside the body to further represent his age.

In this classroom example students embodied characters whose backgrounds were different from their own, including characters with different skin colors, from different age groups, from different socioeconomic backgrounds, and from different neighborhoods, experiencing how the characters' psychology influenced several aspects of their behavior. In addition to meeting the disciplinary goal of encouraging students to reflect on multiple aspects of the human experience, such as death and friendship, these lessons also supported Shirley's students in fostering multimodal representational competence as they considered how the same trait—for instance, old age or bossiness—could be communicated through writing, body movements, and images. By comparing and contrasting each person's physical gestures to the written descriptions of their character traits in a book, Shirley's students also met national standards that require students to compare written literature to visual and embodied literature (see Textbox 3.3).

> **TEXTBOX 3.3**
>
> **CCSS.ELA-Literacy.RL.6.7**
>
> Compare and contrast the experience of reading a story, drama, or poem to listening to or viewing an audio, video, or live version of the text, including contrasting what they "see" and "hear" when reading the text to what they perceive when they listen or watch.

In addition to increasing students' MRC, Shirley supported students' comprehension through applying the strategy of summarizing. In assigning the body biographies, Shirley in effect asked students to summarize the important attributes of the character in a visual form; in requiring students to strike a pose, she required students to summarize the character's attributes in an embodied form. We also can imagine English teachers asking students to summarize scenes or concepts in the manner they feel would be the most compelling, including through producing embodied representations, images, or physical models, and to explain how these representations sum up important aspects of particular poems, memoirs, or other literary and informational works. If transforming one mode to another mode leads to new and generative understandings (Siegel, 1995), then allowing students to summarize their understandings of literature through multiple modes can support their comprehension on symbolic and embodied levels.

This example also illustrates how teachers can support students in conducting close readings of a different kind of text: body language. In the previous examples, Kathryn and John primarily focused their students' attention on other modes, such as images, music, written language, and verbal speech. Body movements, however, are also used in many visual genres to communicate aspects of people's characters, and they, too, can be an imporant source of information for making inferences. Shirley's students made these kinds of inferences when their peers got "in character" and they inferred who they were by their body language. Students further reflected on how body movements conveyed implicit messages when they selected a defining pose for their characters in the body biography and explained how this pose related to the other images, symbols, and words representing the character.

Other Applications of MRC with Embodied Representations

Shirley's students produced embodied representations in conjunction with a young adult novel, but many other English teachers seek to interpret and produce embodied modes in conjunction with playscripts. Celeste, for example, sought to develop her students' MRC with embodied modes when she showed several photographs of the same Shakespearean scenes and asked students to assume the role of directors by identifying the body language they would have recommended to the actors for that particular scene. In one lesson Celeste showed images from plays and movies that depicted Demetrius rebuffing Helena in *A Midsummer Night's Dream*, all of which featured different physical postures: Helena lying on the ground holding on to Demetrius's legs; pulling his arm toward her while he walked the other way; or kneeling beside him as he sat on a rock looking at her. As students discussed the scenes, they noted that some body postures made Helena seem more desperate and distressed than others. After viewing how actors had portrayed Helena, each group decided how they would have portrayed her in a way that fit with the written text, yet moved beyond the written text by implying additional aspects of her emotional state and character. In other words, students made inferences about a written text by identifying which body postures most fully fit the character as they understood her.

Although students in English/language arts are often expected to communicate their understandings through writing essays, we assert that body movements are also a powerful means through which humans express their identities and experience the world, and ELA teachers' instruction can consciously incorporate this mode into their instruction in addition to writing and other modes. As the examples in this section suggest, students can make inferences about literature based on characters' body postures, and they can summarize literary texts through embodied performances. These modified comprehension strategies, in addition to enhancing students' understandings of literature, also build students' multimodal representational competence as they use specific features of embodied representations (e.g., downcast head) to support inferences, which is one aspect of MRC. Transforming written literature into embodied representations (and vice versa) also gives students practice with another aspect of MRC, transforming one mode to another. In other words, comprehension strategies complement MRC in building students' comprehension and production of multimodal, embodied texts.

MULTIMODAL REPRESENTATIONAL COMPETENCE AND PERSUASIVE COMPOSITIONS

While literary genres are large components of English/language arts curricula, another major strand in ELA standards addresses argumentative writing and persuasive writing. Just as the genre of written narratives can be expanded to include the production of multimodal digital narratives, the genre of persuasive essays can be expanded to include the production of multimodal texts as well. Milly, who taught science and math, sought to support her students in producing multimodal persuasive compositions by centering one unit around *public service announcements* (PSAs), defined loosely as texts whose purpose is to raise people's awareness about a pressing issue and to effect changes in people's behavior in relation to that issue. The unit focused on the persuasive techniques used to influence mass audiences on controversial subjects. For their culminating projects, students produced a digital, multimodal PSA regarding an issue that was important to them or to members of their community. This assignment gave them practice with national standards regarding digital text production (see Textbox 3.4).

> **TEXTBOX 3.4**
>
> **CCSS.ELA. W.8.6**
>
> Use technology, including the Internet, to produce and publish writing and present the relationships between information and ideas efficiently as well as to interact and collaborate with others.

To begin this unit on PSAs, Milly showed several popular YouTube videos whose purpose was to raise awareness about a social or environmental issue, influence people's attitudes regarding that issue, or change people's behavior. These videos included the trailer for a documentary on global warming as well as a PSA promoting railway safety. The following vignette illustrates how Milly supported her students in considering how multimodal techniques—including but not limited to verbal language—worked together to persuade viewers to adopt a different attitude or to take a different course of action.

Milly's students begin to watch "Dumb Ways to Die," a PSA sponsored by Metro Trains Melbourne, which features smiling, brightly colored, oblong cartoon characters who "die" due to different causes and subsequently dance to cheerful music. In a Freeze Frame activity, Milly stops the video at two different points. During each pause, students work in small groups to discuss what they see and hear in the video. A printed discussion sheet displays screenshots of the video as well as printed copies of the lyrics. Students are encouraged to annotate these lyrics and images while discussing guided questions such as the following:

- What do you observe about the music at this point in the PSA? Please consider the content of the lyrics, the voice of the singer, and the overall mood of the song.
- What do you notice about the visual representation in this frame of the PSA? Please consider the color and form of the displayed image.
- Select one part of the PSA at this point in time and change one aspect about it (voice of singer; type of music; type of image, and so on). Be prepared to discuss how changing one mode of representation would affect the tone or meaning of the PSA.

After the PSA ends, the students hold an additional small-group discussion and address questions such as:

- Why do you think McCann Melbourne, the advertising company, chose these forms of representation in its safety message as opposed to the alternatives you listed above?
- This video is a public safety message promoting railway safety. What did you notice about the organization of this video? Why do you think McCann Melbourne organized it that way?
- This video has been viewed over 46 million times, has reduced railway accidents in Melbourne by 30%, and (according to Wikipedia) has been called "Australia's biggest ever viral hit." Why do you think this PSA was so persuasive and successful?
- Any other overall insights about the video?

After students finish their discussions, Milly asks, "What did you talk about in your small groups?"

"[The PSA is] really edgy," responds one student. "We talked about changing the music to heavy metal music, but that would cross the line of being too edgy. The heavy metal would make the video too threatening for people."

"You talked about changing the music to heavy metal music," Milly responds. "So what about the music currently in the ad?"

"The voice is like a younger girl's voice."

"And it's happy."

"Okay, so it's not threatening, like Greg said," Milly repeats. "People can still accept the video, even with that dark message, because it's not threatening with the girl's voice and the happy music. But with heavy metal music, the PSA could seem too threatening. What else makes the video not threatening?"

"It starts out with a sunny day."

"And the cartoons look like dancing jellybeans."

"Why is that nonthreatening?," asks Milly.

"It makes it seem less real."

"They're still dancing after they get killed. If it was real humans, they'd be hurt and it wouldn't be funny."

"So it goes back to being nonthreatening. If the video had real humans, it would be too dark. I actually found another parody video that shows real people doing these things, like poking a grizzly bear and stepping in front of a train." Milly shows a few scenes from the YouTube parody and then stops.

"Why didn't you play the whole thing?" one student asks.

"I want to keep my job."

"Oh yeah, because you don't want to show people's privates getting eaten by piranas [one of the ways a 'jellybean character' died]."

"Yeah, the actual video footage of humans gives it a whole different feeling, doesn't it? It's much more graphic. I felt comfortable playing the cartoon but not the actual footage. What other things did you talk about in your groups?"

"It didn't even seem like a public service announcement. They didn't mention getting hit by trains until the very end."

"Why does that make it effective?," asks Milly.

"Because you just think it's a funny cartoon and then at the end you realize it has a message. So it doesn't seem like it's about train safety until the very end," the student responds.

"It's not like preaching or telling you to do something," another student rejoins.

"Yeah, that reminds me, the head of the advertising agency said, [Milly clicks on a website and reads from the page] 'The aim of this campaign is to engage an audience that really doesn't want to hear any kind of safety message.' So the video's organization of waiting until the end to even mention railway safety kind of accomplishes that goal."

In this example Milly fostered her students' multimodal representational competence as they explained the relationship between two or more modes that communicated the same message. Specifically, students discussed the relationship among modes that appeared within the same PSA. As students contrasted the video footage versus the cartoons depicting the same events, they also explored how one type of representation (cartoons) was more fitting to meet a particular purpose than another type of representation (video footage), which is another aspect of MRC.

These aspects of MRC relate closely to the comprehension strategy of making connections. Previous scholars (Beers, 2003) have noted that the strategy of making connections in ELA includes making "within text" connections. For example, when reading a novel, students can note how a particular symbol appears in multiple sections, using these instances to speculate on the symbol's significance to the work as a whole. When interpreting and producing multimodal texts, by contrast, these "within text" connections not only include comparing and contrasting the same text at different points in time, but also making connections across different modes at the same point in time.

Milly's students made these types of connections in their analysis of the PSA when Milly paused it at several points for the Freeze Frame activity. At each point in time, students noted how the cartoons, the upbeat music, and the young girl's voice were all congruous. That is, the bright colors; the smiling, dancing jelly-bean forms; the simple rhymes; the girl's voice; and the music all portrayed an upbeat tone that seemed appropriate for children. However, the content of the lyrics—the gruesome ways to die—was dark and seemingly at odds with the bright, happy forms. They speculated that these contrasting modes were used by the advertisers to make a decidedly serious message—"Don't step onto an active railway or you might die"—into a playful message that was easier to accept. In other words, by making connections across different modes, students were able to identify how the characteristics of the PSA contributed to an overall tone and message.

In addition to assisting students in making mode-to-mode connections within the same PSA, Milly also sought to guide her students in making text-to-text connections when they noted similarities and differences across two YouTube videos with the "same" message. By showing how this PSA had an entirely different tone when just one mode changed, Milly encouraged students to identify how changes in representation can affect meaning. We imagine that other English teachers can accomplish similar goals through discussing multiple representations of the same phenomenon, identifying which one they would choose for a particular audience and purpose, and justifying their answers. The following vignette points toward other ways in which Milly sought to develop her students' multimodal literacy throughout the unit on persuasive compositions.

After students watch "Dumb Ways to Die," Milly shows other models of PSAs, such as the trailer for the documentary *An Inconvenient Truth*, whose purpose is to raise awareness about global warming and to effect change in policy and individual behavior. Photographs of destroyed buildings, as well as videos of people crying over deceased loved ones, are paired with a deep, melodramatic voice stating, "A film that has shocked audiences everywhere they've seen it." Symphony music comes to an increasing crescendo, which reaches its peak as Al Gore verbally concludes, "Our ability to live is what is at stake." As in the first video, students likewise note the forms of representation and techniques used in this trailer, including the quality of the voice, the word choice in the written phrases, the decision to frame the PSA with Gore speaking in a lecture hall, the selection and juxtaposition of photographs and line graphs, and so forth.

To prepare for writing their own PSAs, Milly poses questions in which students "quick write" about problems they notice in the school, community, and world. Students also select a member of their school or community, and conduct an interview about problems they are facing. After selecting and researching a problem and deciding on the audience they would like to reach, students make storyboards of PSAs in which they identify the music, tone of voice, and forms of visual representation they would like to persuade their given audience. Much as Kathryn's students did, they then use the storyboards to produce multimodal PSAs on topics such as not texting while driving and being accepting of people with mental illness.

Milly's students then explain why they chose particular forms of representation (e.g., happy or sad music, photographs or cartoons, verbal narration by people affected by the issue versus verbal narration by a deep voice, and so on). Sonia, for instance, chooses two real human actors for her antibullying PSA (see Figure 3.1 for the first frame of her storyboard), which ends with a close-up of Alan's tear-streaked face after Roger had shoved him into his locker. She explains to Milly that she designed the close framing of the final shot, as well as the realism of the video, to make viewers feel sorry for Alan as they recognized the real human consequences of bullying. She also explains she chose a dark color for the lockers to portray a feeling of sadness.

In this example Milly worked to build several aspects of students' multimodal representational competence while simultaneously meeting the disciplinary goal of using various techniques to persuade an audience. One aspect of MRC is the ability to "select, combine, and/or produce representations in ways that effectively communicate disciplinary concepts." Milly supported students in consciously and strategically selecting representations while considering questions such as the following:

- What audience would you like to reach with your PSA?
- What overall tone would you like your PSA to convey?
- For this particular issue, would your audience be more persuaded by a deep voice, by a child's voice, or by another voice? Please explain your answer.

FIGURE 3.1. Sonia's storyboard for her antibullying PSA.

- Would your audience be more persuaded by one genre of music than another? Please explain your answer.
- Would your audience be more persuaded by line graphs, by scientific representations, by cartoons, by photographs, or by another type of visual representation? Please explain your answer.

This component of MRC can dovetail with the comprehension strategy of making inferences. Much as Kathryn's students used the characteristics of images to make inferences about the identity of the artists, Milly's students used the characteristics of images to make inferences about the advertiser's persuasive approach. Students also made inferences or predictions about what kinds of multimodal characteristics would be likely to have the desired effect on their intended audience.

One such characteristic that students can study is each image's orientation. Image-makers tend to assume one of three general orientations toward the subjects of their images (Wilson & Landon-Hays, in press). First, images with naturalistic orientations seek to portray the world "as it is" in a manner that aligns with humans' everyday perceptions, such as through photographs and video footage. Second, schematic images often assume a scientific or mathematical orientation toward knowledge, often with the intention of explaining a phenomenon. Under this definition, examples of schematics include line graphs and diagrams. Third, images can have an aesthetic orientation toward knowledge, such as in fanciful illustrations, artwork, and cartoons. Sometimes, the subjects of these images do not exist in an external reality, such as dancing and smiling jelly beans.

Noticing whether images are aesthetic, naturalistic, and/or schematic can help students identify the method by which the text-maker seeks to persuade the audience. "Dumb Ways to Die," for example, could have featured real video footage of trains, coupled with bar graphs illustrating the number of deaths from train accidents each year. Indeed, the trailer for *An Inconvenient Truth* took that approach by juxtaposing schematic images, seemingly adding scientific legitimacy, and naturalistic images, seemingly depicting the world exactly as it is. By contrast, "Dumb Ways to Die" was exaggerated in the degree to which the characters were depicted as not existing in an external reality. This use of aesthetically oriented images indicated that the makers of the PSA for railway saftey were using a different method of persuasion (aesthetically oriented comedy) than the makers of the trailer against global warming.

Closely related to the concept of *orientation* is the concept of *modality*. In essence, modality is the "truth value" ascribed to any image (Halliday, 1973; Kress & van Leeuwen, 2006); in other words, modality is a gauge of whether the image is supposed to be taken as true, factual, and objective, or whether it is supposed to be taken as a questionable statement, personal belief, or product of the author's imagination. In writing, lower modality is established through statements such as "It is *probably* true that," "It is *likely* that," or "She *believed* that," whereas statements without these markers connote a higher degree of certainty (e.g., Burning fossil fuels contributes to global warming).

Just as writers use techniques to indicate the questionability of their statements, image-makers likewise create images with higher or lower degrees of modality, but they use orientation to do so. Although photographs can be photoshopped, for instance, their provenance includes the historical documentation of events or phenomena that are presumed to exist in an external, perceptually visible world. Scientific diagrams have authoritatively explained or illustrated allegedly objective processes. By contrast, many works of art are visibly and overtly the product of an artist's creativity, imagination, and distinctly subjective vision. As students choose whether to persuade somebody using photographs, illustrations, diagrams, or other types of images, therefore, they can make inferences about which orientation is most likely to persuade their intended audience and use that orientation to align with their overall strategy of persuasion.

Critical Literacy in English/Language Arts

Through this type of instruction, Milly promoted critical literacy on two fronts: first, by teaching students to analyze multimodal texts more critically and consciously; and second, through using students' own multimodal texts to promote social change. At other times, she sought to accomplish the same objective through other means. For instance, her students placed magazine ads into groups based on their similarities and then gave each group a label. Some students formed groups of "food for men" and "food for women," noting that men's advertisements used words such as "power," often featured meat and or other proteins, and included bold colors such as reds and blacks. By contrast, the group labeled "food for women" was more likely to feature lighter backgrounds with children, families, or friends eating together. After discussing the persuasive techniques used in these ads, students chose one group of advertisements and made an ad with a countermessage—for example, depicting a man eating "light and healthy" food with his family against a pastel background.

As demonstrated in these examples, one method for teaching multimodal critical literacy in language arts includes selecting "community texts" or texts from popular media and analyzing how the authors' techniques communicate assumptions about their values, positions, beliefs, and purposes. In the words of Luke, O'Brien, and Comber (1994), these questions can include:

- How is (this topic) being presented? What themes and discourses are being used?
- Who is writing to whom? Whose voices and positions are being expressed?
- Whose voices and positions are not being expressed?
- What is the text trying to do to you?
- What other ways are there of writing (and representing) about the topic?
- What wasn't said about the topic, and why? (p. 143)

Asking these types of questions can encourage students to be more aware of how people convey implicit assumptions in the multimodal texts that surround them; these types of questions also meet national standards that emphasize critical media literacy (see Textbox 3.5). "Talking back" to multimodal texts through countermessages enables students to join digital and community conversations more purposefully and strategically (Luke, O'Brien, & Comber, 1994).

> **TEXTBOX 3.5**
>
> **CCSS.ELA.SL.8.2**
>
> Analyze the purpose of information presented in diverse media and formats (e.g., visually, quantitatively, orally) and evaluate the motives (e.g., social, commercial, political) behind its presentation.

For other researchers (Seely-Flint & Laman, 2012), critical literacy in English is less about questioning messages related to power and the positioning of particular social groups, and more about allowing students to express themselves regarding substantive topics that are important to them, using media that are important to them. We believe that Kathryn took this approach when she allowed her students to select music they liked, to speak and write in both Spanish and English, and to select images of foods, places, and people they loved. We can imagine this kind of literacy extending itself to students who like to express themselves through other media as well, such as through hip-hop and embodied performance (Hill, 2009), or through grass dancing and Native regalia (Wilson & Boatright, 2011). Indeed, allowing students to interpret, critique, produce, and evaluate a wide variety of multimodal texts based on their preferences may be central to critical literacy instruction that accounts for students' cultural backgrounds.

SUPPORTING MULTIMODAL LITERACY THROUGH THINK-ALOUDS

Teachers and researchers have long recommended think-alouds as a means for building students' comprehension. In traditional think-alouds on printed texts, teachers usually project an excerpt from a text on an interactive whiteboard and they annotate it as they make connections, make inferences, ask questions, and verbally articulate other comprehension strategies. In addition to using these general comprehension strategies during think-alouds, teachers also use discipline-specific frameworks to evaluate and critique texts. For instance, English teachers might articulate their thoughts on how a particular rhyme scheme influenced the tone of a poem or how a particular organizational statement shaped their expectations for the rest of an essay.

Think-alouds are based on the assumption that advanced practitioners have developed frameworks for interpreting texts, which may not be immediately evident to novices. By making their thinking visible, teachers apprentice students into reading and evaluating texts more proficiently. Under a gradual release model, these teacher-led think-alouds would be followed by repeated opportunities for students to independently apply similar strategies themselves through think-alouds or annotations.

How might think-alouds be modified to account for the unique nature of multimodal texts in English? Milly's discussion surrounding "Dumb Ways to Die" points toward ways in which English teachers can help students become more proficient readers of multimodal texts. We can imagine Milly showing the initial YouTube page to her students and modeling how she used its text features—such as the title of the video, the name of the agency that posted the video, and the image of the smiling jelly bean—to make predictions about the purpose, tone, audience, and message of the PSA.

While playing the video, Milly could confirm or revise these initial predictions using multimodal features, for instance, through saying, "The high-pitched voice of the singer, which sounds like a young woman's voice, confirms my initial prediction that this video is trying to appeal to a younger audience." We imagine part of this think-aloud would include noting congruities and incongruities across modes as Milly noted that happy cartoons "matched" with the upbeat music but did not "match" with the message that playing near railways has led to death and injury. Finally, Milly could model the process of making inferences about why the agency chose to present the message in the way that it did, as well as inferences about why the PSA was so successful for the targeted audience and whether or not it would be as successful with other audiences.

As suggested by this example, think-alouds on multimodal texts are often similar to think-alouds on printed texts, with the exception that teachers must also consider how a variety of visual and aural features affect the overall tone, theme, or organization of the work. Questions or prompts for student think-alouds on multimodal texts can include the following:

- What implicit values or positions are communicated, and how are they communicated through music, body movements, image orientation, color, or other multimodal features?
- How might somebody with a different set of values or positions communicate the same topic through music, body movements, image orientation, color, or other multimodal features?
- How did the intended audience of the text influence the text-makers' choice of representations?
- What are the text-makers trying to get me to do or trying to make me feel? What techniques do they use to accomplish this goal?
- What is the implied social relationship evident in this text? How does the text-maker establish this social relationship?
- Where have I seen or heard similar images, body movements, accents, or types of music before? What is the effect of this provenance on the meaning of the text?
- If I changed the provenance of the text (e.g., chose music that is historically from Mexico versus music that historically came from the southeastern United States), how might that change the meaning of the overall text?
- If I changed one of the modes in another way (e.g., from a photograph to a cartoon), how might that change the meaning of the overall text?
- In what ways do different modes align with each other, and in what ways do they seem to be at odds with each other?
- I infer, based on . . . , that . . . (e.g., I infer, based on the distant framing and lack of eye contact, that the text-maker may not want me to feel personally connected to this subject).
- I predict, based on . . . that . . . (e.g., I predict, based on the initial sunny image, that this video will be about a happy topic).

Just as students can become more strategic and critical readers of printed texts, so too they can become more discerning readers of multimodal texts through observing practiced readers in action and through trying similar approaches themselves. These student and teacher think-alouds can synthesize many of the techniques highlighted throughout this chapter as people make inferences about why the text-makers selected images with artistic or schematic orientations, or as they make connections to previous instances in which they have heard/seen similar modes in order to determine the text's cultural/historical connotations. These types of think-alouds would support students' application of comprehension strategies, as well as develop their multimodal representational competence.

CHAPTER INSIGHTS

One primary goal of English/language arts has long been to teach students to communicate powerfully for purposes that matter to them. Although historically much communication was accomplished orally or in print, new technologies have changed the landscape of ELA as teachers seek to support their students in interpreting and producing a wide array of multimodal digital communications. Teachers can accomplish this task through leading discussions regarding how particular modes—including music, tonal quality, image types, and other features—work together to produce overall effects. Students can also produce their own multimodal texts, justify why they selected particular modes, and explain the effects they hoped multimodal techniques would have on their viewers. This type of instruction can help students develop multimodal representational competence as well as enhance their understandings of core disciplinary concepts and standards.

CHAPTER 4

Reading and Representing in Mathematics

Mathematics is foundational to people's lives as individuals and as members of society. Whether people are measuring batter, negotiating the terms of a loan, interpreting sports statistics, or calculating the probability of winning a card game, mathematical reasoning can be applied to a host of pragmatic, professional, and recreational situations, enabling people to make informed decisions, large and small. Representations are often central to this process of decision making by helping people clarify their thinking about numbers and space. Because calculations can be difficult for people to make in their heads, a host of numeric, written, and visual representations can help them ensure accuracy as they reason through everyday problems.

To counter historically prevalent methods of teaching mathematics as a series of known procedures and representations, the National Council of Teachers of Mathematics (NCTM, 2000) has recommended an approach to mathematics education in which *problem solving* and *representation* play central roles, an approach that has been echoed in the Common Core State Standards (CCSS; National Governors Association Center for Best Practices & Council of Chief State School Officers, 2010). As proficient students encounter or formulate problems of their own, they know how to generate and use multiple representations—such as standard and nonstandard images, manipulatives, graphs, and numbers/symbols—which help them reason through the problem. Under this problem-solving approach, students reason abstractly and flexibly about *numbers* (including their operations and relations) and *space,* recognizing that they are not contained within any one representation or method, but are accessible through many (Hoffman, Lenhard, & Seeger, 2005).

This type of mathematics instruction seeks to foster *conceptual understanding,* which the National Research Council (2001; cf. National Governors Association Center for Best Practices & Council of Chief State School Officers, 2010) has asserted is a major goal of mathematics education. Conceptual understanding can be accomplished in many different ways. Take the case of dividing by fractions, for instance. Instead of simply listening to instructions on how to "invert and multiply" the second fraction, students can share what they know about division of whole numbers and use that knowledge as a springboard to discuss division of fractions, identify instances when they might have to divide fractions as they split wholes or parts into pieces, and use manipulatives or images to devise their own algorithm. Researchers (diSessa, 2004; Roth, 2004) have suggested that asking students to develop and compare their own representations before showing them conventional representations—for instance, asking them to develop prototypes of line graphs before showing them formal line graphs—often leads to deeper conceptual understanding of mathematical ideas.

At the same time, while developing conceptual understanding is a core goal of mathematics, so too is developing procedural fluency and efficiency. Thus, not only is generating one's own representations and methods for solving problems an indispensable component of mathematical reasoning, but it is also important to know how to apply familiar and efficient algorithms and formulas, how to use conventional representations that have been honed over time, and how to use technologies that expedite processes of representation and computation.

Although a student may develop her own prototype of a line graph or his own image for dividing fractions, there are reasons why people use Cartesian coordinate planes and conventional numerals and symbols for fractions: They are efficient and precise for what they do, and communities of mathematicians can understand them. Mathematics instruction at its best, then, can solicit student-generated representations, solutions, and definitions while comparing them to those established by mathematical communities, helping students develop conceptual understandings while familiarizing them with the conventions of mathematics.

Another important component of mathematical proficiency is *metacognition,* or the active regulation of one's thinking as one solves problems (Desoete & Veenman, 2006; National Council of Teachers of Mathematics, 2000). Metacognitive students approach a problem strategically, comparing it to simpler but similar problems they have solved, using familiar "benchmark" numbers to estimate answers, looking for patterns and regularities in the representations they are using, and constantly asking themselves if their answers make sense. They are likewise able to communicate these thought processes to others through modes such as verbal explanations, written explanations, numeric explanations, images, graphs, and manipulatives. Through these informal proofs or argumentations, they can explain why they arrived at particular answers and how their conclusions compare to those that are accepted in mathematical communities.

Thus the discipline of mathematics requires students to work with a highly articulated system of abstractions that are both generalizable and applicable to specific situations. Over time, mathematicians have developed representations, definitions, and procedures in relation to these abstractions. Although students can devise their own representations, generalizations, and procedures as they build understandings of new concepts, mathematical proficiency also requires students to read and use established representations, generalizations, and procedures and understand the relationships between them. Students can apply mathematical reasoning to many situations that impact their quality of life in large and small ways as individuals, as consumers, as professionals, and as citizens.

SYMBOLS AND SPEECH: DEVELOPING REPRESENTATIONAL COMPETENCE WITH NUMBERS IN MATHEMATICS

Multimodal representational competence commonly addresses transformations across modes: transforming numeric tables to graphs, three-dimensional models to two-dimensional images, and more. While this component of MRC is certainly central to mathematics, so, too, are "within mode" transformations as students transform one numeric/symbolic representation (NSR) to another. For instance, although the NSRs $5\frac{1}{8}$, $6\frac{6}{16}$, and 6.375 can all accurately represent the same quantity, some students may not recognize they are equivalent, or they may not be able to explain how one number can be "changed" into another. Moreover, even when students can fluently make transformations across NSRs, they may have difficulty in selecting the NSR that best fits their needs, in terms of whether its spatial arrangement enables them to perform a particular operation and in terms of whether that NSR would be appropriate and useful in a particular context.

The vignette below describes how Grace sought to develop her students' representational competence by selecting the right NSR for the right situation, as well as by guiding them in transforming one NSR into another.

Grace introduces a word problem in which two local basketball teams are tied at the final buzzer. Caught up in the intense rivalry, the coach of the visiting team steps onto the court just as the buzzer sounds, causing the referee to call a technical foul. Students, acting as the assistant coach, must present a speech to their head coach in which they advise her regarding which player should be selected to make the final free throw based on the number of free throws she had made throughout the season. Grace begins a conversation about which player they should recommend to their head coach.

"Angela made 12 out of 15 free throws; Emily made 15 out of 20 free throws; Christina made 13 out of 16 free throws. Who's the best free throw shooter here?" Grace asks.

"Christina, because I thought that she missed three. And Emily, she struck 15 out of 20, she missed five," one student explains.

"You want Christina who missed three over Angela who missed three? But Angela and Christina missed the same number. They both missed three. What do you think, Rico?"

"Emily, because she made the most shots."

Another student offers, "I think I would pick Angela because she might have tried the least amount, but she got, um . . . [silence]"

"It's kind of hard to explain, isn't it," Grace says.

"I think Emily because even though she missed the most, she got fifteen shots though, that's still more than anyone else. And she got all sweaty and stuff, and she was tired by the end."

Grace responds, "It's kind of hard to pick who would be the absolute best free throw shooter. Is there any other way we could look at it? Besides looking at the actual number they got and the actual number they missed?"

"Look at the number they tried."

"We could look at the number they tried. So if I only tried three shots, but I made three out of three, I might be the best free throw shooter," Grace agrees. "Can I write these as fractions? Go ahead and write the fractions you would put for each of these girls. Now that we've got them written as fractions, can you tell who is the best free throw shooter?"

Students sit in silence for a minute, and shake heads no.

"Let me ask you this. If they all made 20 shots, if they all shot the ball 20 times, if they all attempted 20 times, would you be able to tell then who was the best free throw shooter? If they had all done 20, how would you know who was the best free throw shooter?"

"Who had the most shots."

Prompted by Grace's suggestion that if the players had all made the same number of shots, the students could tell who was the best, one student suggests, "Find the lowest common denominator."

"How would that help us?" asks Grace.

"If all of the bottom numbers were the same, you could look at the top numbers to see who made the most shots."

Students agree that this approach would provide a fairer comparison, and they try to use the lowest common denominator to provide evidence for their speech to the head coach. After they decide to change each fraction into equivalent fractions with 80 as the denominator, Grace asks them if they should tell the coach that Christina would make about 65 out of 80 shots while the others would make about 60 or 64 out of 80 shots. "Do we know that Christina would make 65 out of 80 shots? Is that what we should say to the head coach?"

Students agree that they don't know for sure that Christina would make 65 out of 80 shots if she repeatedly shot the ball, but one student offers, "You could tell the percent of shots that she made."

"You could tell her the percent of shots that each player made." Grace echoes. "So we don't know if the player keeps on shooting, if she will actually make 65 out of 80 shots, but we can figure out the percent of shots that she already made."

Throughout this discussion, Grace supported her students in developing one aspect of MRC (see "Multimodal Representational Competence Across Disciplines" in Chapter 1), identifying when one representation is more apt for a particular purpose than another one, when she required students to use the NSR that would be the most persuasive and appropriate in their speech to the head coach. Although the NSRs $65/80$, $64/80$, and $60/80$ enabled students to accurately tell the coach who was the best shooter, these NSRs were not conventional for this particular situation. Instead, students identified that percentages, rather than equivalent fractions, would be the most sensible NSR in this particular instance. In this way, Grace encouraged students to consider how particular NSRs can be selected based on context, rather than selected based solely on accuracy.

This aspect of MRC may often be tied to the comprehension strategy of inferring, as students are faced with scenarios that can be found in real-life settings and have to make inferences about which approach would be best within each setting. Often, when students apply mathematical knowledge in professional and personal settings outside of school, the

---

TEXTBOX 4.1

NCTM Communication Standards for Grades 6–8

Instructional programs should enable all students to

» organize and consolidate their mathematical thinking through communication;

» communicate their mathematical thinking coherently and clearly to peers, teachers, and others;

» analyze and evaluate the mathematical thinking and strategies of others;

» use the language of mathematics to express mathematical ideas precisely.

---

problems they face are "ill-structured" in the sense that there are many ways to address the problems and there are several possible solutions to each problem (Jonassen, 2000). For instance, there are multiple factors to consider while selecting an interest rate and duration of a loan, and the consideration of these factors leads different people to make different decisions that can all result in financial stability. Furthermore, problems with no predetermined pathway are often encountered in STEM-related professions (Jonassen, 1997).

Accordingly, mathematics teachers can provide students with situations in which they have to make their own inferences about how they might structure and present data to meet the demands of a particular situation, an approach that would help students to meet the standards in Textbox 4.1. In this vignette the stated scenario—"give a speech to persuade the head coach"—did not specify the method by which students should convince the coach. Students' speeches could have argued, for instance, that either Christina or Angela would have been a reasonable selection given that one made only 1.25% more shots than the other.

Rather than predetermining the manner in which students should structure their argument, or rather than assuming that there was only one correct argument to make, Grace instead supported her students in making inferences about what they thought the coach would like to hear. These inferences included using their past experiences with basketball games to infer which type of numeric/symbolic representation or claim would be most appropriate for this particular context. In this sense, the comprehension strategy of making inferences and the fourth aspect of MRC ("select representations that are apt for particular purposes") worked together to enhance students' ability to apply mathematical reasoning to contextualized situations.

Grace supported her students in applying a second comprehension strategy as well: Her students made predictions about who would be the best free throw shooter before confirming or rejecting their predictions mathematically. In this case, several players were almost evenly matched, making an accurate prediction difficult, but in many other cases, this strategy of predicting/checking predictions enables students to catch simple computational errors that caused the answer to be far off from their original predictions. To further enhance students' thinking in this lesson, Grace could ask students to revisit their original predictions at the end of the lesson and explain why they were right or wrong. For instance, one student might say, "I thought Emily would be the best player because she made the most shots, but the best player was really Christina because she made a greater percentage of shots that she tried."

In the next vignette Grace continued her lesson by prompting students on how they might actually figure out the percentages so that they could report them to the coach.

> "How could we figure out the percent?"
>
> After a moment of silence, Grace asks, "What does *percent* mean?"
>
> "It means that it's out of hundredths."
>
> "So can I represent any of these fractions as out of hundredths?" Grace asks as she points to the numerals $12/15$, $15/20$, and $13/16$ on the whiteboard. Grace's students use their knowledge of equivalent fractions to show that $15/20 = 75/100$, or 75%.
>
> A student then asks, "You know how you want to get 100 for the denominator? What if you had a number like 30 in the denominator?"
>
> "Let's make it something like seventeen-thirtieths," Grace says, and writes $17/30$ on board. "Think about what this line means (points to line between the numerator and the denominator). What does it mean to do?"
>
> "Divide."
>
> Grace asks students to work in small groups to use what they know to see if they can determine the percentage of shots that Christina and Angela made. A few groups use division to obtain decimals, then use what they stated about decimals and percentages at the beginning of the lesson to change each decimal to a percentage. One group sets up the problem as equivalent fractions, writing that $13/16 = ?/100$, and uses cross multiplication to arrive at a percentage. Each group explains their solution to the class, then works together to write a brief speech to the head coach explaining why Christina should be selected to make the final free throw shot.

In this latter half of the lesson Grace fostered her students' representational competence in a different way: by supporting them in transforming one representation (NSRs written as fractions) to another (NSRs written as percentages). Students also applied the comprehension strategy of summarizing as they verbally recounted how they accomplished their transformations from fractions to percentages.

Researchers (e.g., Connolly & Vilardi, 1989) have argued that written and spoken language provide a "metadiscourse" in mathematics, in the sense that people can use them to describe NSRs and other representations. Requiring students to verbally explain their reasoning can therefore solidify and strengthen their understandings of mathematical processes and concepts because in the process of verbally explaining something to others, students often clarify for themselves what they mean (e.g., Fogelberg et al., 2008). We argue that this comprehension strategy of verbally summarizing also supports MRC when students summarize how they transformed one representation into another, as in this lesson.

Finally, this instructional example illustrates that the comprehension strategy of asking questions can be applied to multiple representations. In this case, one student asked how he could transform fractions to percentages in cases where the original fraction did not have denominators that could be equivalent to hundredths. Although he asked this question without prompting, one could imagine Grace further supporting this comprehension strategy by stopping the discussion at strategic points and allowing students to write questions they had about the targeted concepts. For instance, Grace could ask students to write questions they still had about fractions, decimals, and percentages at the beginning of this lesson (e.g., How are decimals different from fractions? How can you change fractions to percentages?). Grace could post a few key questions on the whiteboard, and return to them after the unit was over to make sure they had been answered.

We argue that the strategy of asking questions is especially important in mathematics, a discipline in which many students have questions about concepts and procedures but do not feel comfortable asking them in front of the class for fear of "looking dumb." Alternatively, many students misunderstand mathematical concepts or situations, but they are not aware that their understandings are incomplete. To address these issues, requiring students to ask questions can help students realize that they do not understand something and also give them structured opportunities to address their questions in ways that do not make them "look dumb" in front of their peers. In other words, the comprehension strategy of asking questions can promote more accurate or richer understandings of numerical and visual texts just as they can promote deeper understandings of written texts when students make their questions explicit and discuss them with others.

Other Applications of MRC with Symbols and Speech

The comprehension strategies used in this example held wide application beyond this individual lesson as Grace assisted her students in understanding and transforming NSRs throughout the school year. To reinforce the comprehension strategy of summarizing, Grace often required students to summarize their work aloud, and she repeatedly encouraged precision with their mathematical terminology. For instance, when one student read 15^3 as "15 with a 3," Grace asked him to clarify what he meant, to which he responded, "15 times 3." Grace's students then speculated on other ways they could have read this, including "15 times 15 times 15," "15 cubed," and "15 with an exponent of 3," and they identified which verbal expressions meant the same thing as 15^3 and which meant something different. By creating a *verbal culture* in the classroom—or a place in which students constantly used a variety of ways to verbally summarize mathematical problems and concepts—she further supported their understanding of the meaning of numeric/symbolic representations.

In addition to developing a verbal culture through the spoken word, Grace sought to maintain a verbal culture through writing as well. Thus her students would occasionally read solutions or arguments with mathematical errors in them and would annotate these texts by noting the flaws in the author's reasoning. For instance, her students read a text by a fictitious contractor who told a client that he needed a certain amount of water to fill his swimming pool, a certain amount of chlorine per gallon, and a certain amount of chlorine overall. Students annotated the problem by explaining where his reasoning was flawed, by using NSRs to prove these flaws, and by sharing their annotations with others.

In all, establishing a verbal culture—including a culture where students read and explain NSRs through words and where students prove or disprove written arguments through NSRs—can foster representational competence with numbers. The following sections describe how representational competence with numbers can be connected to a variety of other modes, such as manipulatives, graphs, and drawings.

PICTURING MATHEMATICS: LITERACY INSTRUCTION ON VISUALS

In addition to a variety of NSRs, images also regularly appear in many mathematics classrooms. These images, however, are distinct from those found in many other disciplines. In other disciplines, images often look like the objects they represent, at least to some degree, such as photographs of volcanoes that look like real volcanoes or illustrations of characters that look like the author's description of them. Peirce (1991) called images that look like their referents *iconic*.

In mathematics, however, the purpose behind many disciplinary images is not to look like an externally existing object, but instead to enable people to visualize relationships or to solve problems. Indeed, iconic visuals do not necessarily enhance students' mathematical reasoning (Gray, Pinto, Pitta, & Tall, 1999). Instead, images in mathematics are usually schematic representations, which exclude many iconic elements (e.g., a background landscape) to focus viewers' perceptions only on the details that are relevant to the solution or explanation. Because students' visual displays shape their understandings of problems and influence their conclusions (Miera, 1995), it is important that students learn how to produce visuals that enable them to arrive at reasonable solutions.

This shift from iconic to schematic images took mathematicians several centuries to achieve (O'Halloran, 2005), and many students—relatively new to the conventions of mathematics—often have difficulty in producing images that enable them to visualize relationships or solve problems. Building multimodal representational competence in mathematics therefore includes teaching students how to produce images whose forms can help them reason through problems, as well as explicitly teaching students how to interpret images and their connections to other modes. The following vignette describes how Tracy, who taught science and math, sought to build her students' MRC in relation to mathematical images.

> As students walk into the classroom, the following word problem is on the whiteboard:
> "Naylah plans to make small cheese pizzas to sell at a school fundraiser. She has nine bars of cheese. How many pizzas can she make if each pizza needs the given amount of cheese?"
> Tracy writes ½ bar under the word problem and asks students to use their small whiteboards to draw a visual representing the word

problem. After students draw their pictures in small groups, Tracy asks students to write the problem numerically, making sure that their numeric representation enables them to reach the same solution as their initial visual representation.

"I was really interested in that back group over there," Tracy says after walking around and talking with each group. "I said, well how would you write this problem? And Lorena said she felt like this would be nine times two [Tracy writes 9 x 2 on the front whiteboard], and then Kaitlyn said she thought it would be nine divided by one half [Tracy writes 9½ underneath 9 x 2], but both groups said Naylah can make 18 pizzas. Let's think about that."

Tracy changes the number underneath the word problem to ⅓ bar and then to ⅕ bar, and students again solve the problems by first creating a visual representation and then writing the problem numerically. Tracy writes the students' numeric statements on the board (see Figure 4.1), and students note the pattern that they see emerging in the numbers. Drawing from this pattern, students predict what would happen if Tracy had changed the amount of cheese needed for each pizza to ¼ or ⅙, this time without drawing the visuals.

In this example Tracy fostered the development of at least two aspects of multimodal representational competence. First, students transformed one mode (images) to another mode (numbers), and they made sure that the two modes "said the same thing" in the sense that they both clearly represented the same solution. Tracy insisted, for instance, when one group's NSR said 9 x 2 = 18, then there should be 18 sections highlighted in their visual. Second, students used features of representations to support predictions. Specifically, they used the features of the representation in Figure 4.1 to predict what would happen if the numerals ½, ⅓, and ⅕ were replaced with ¼ and ⅙. In this way, they met the national standard in Textbox 4.2 by noticing and using patterns to make predictions or draw conclusions.

> **TEXTBOX 4.2**
>
> **CCSS.Math.**
> **Practice.MP7**
>
> Look for and make use of structure.
>
> *Mathematically proficient students look closely to discern a pattern or structure.*

These aspects of multimodal representational competence are related to the comprehension strategy of making connections. Students made connections across modes when they compared and contrasted the solutions expressed through their NSR to the solutions expressed through their

FIGURE 4.1. This representation showed patterns in the multiplication and division of fractions.

visual. In her conversations with each individual group, Tracy required students to verbally explain how their visual and numeric representation indicated the same solution. In the case of one group, whose NSR did not match their image, this strategy of making connections across modes enabled them to realize their solution was questionable, and to go back and recheck their work in both modes to see where they had made a mistake.

As illustrated by this example, we believe that making connections across modes also correlates with the comprehension strategy of making and checking predictions. Students can make a prediction through drawing a visual, and they can check their prediction through an NSR, or they can make a prediction through an NSR, and check their prediction through drawing a visual. In both cases, requiring students to produce visuals in addition to NSRs can support them in becoming more proficient mathematical thinkers and communicators as they practice representing the same mathematical concept in multiple ways.

In addition to making and checking predictions by comparing two modes (NSRs and images), Tracy also asked students to make predictions simply by looking at the pattern in Figure 4.1. Using the pattern established through this representation, students predicted that 9 ÷ ⅙ would be the same as 9 x 6. Although this representation is arguably a NSR instead of an "image," we argue that its spatial features—such as the consistent placement of each numeral in the sequence—enabled students to more easily "see" the pattern.

In the vignette below we describe the rest of this lesson in which Tracy continued to support students' multimodal representational competence.

FIGURE 4.2. Deron drew this image to justify his solution to the word problem.

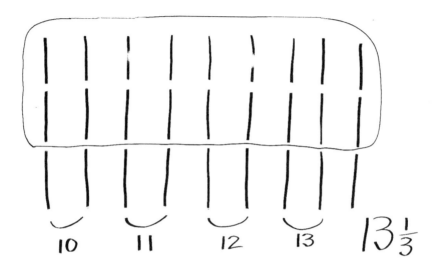

Tracy changes the number on the bottom of the word problem to ⅔ bar, and students again work in groups to draw a visual representing their solutions. Although all groups had previously come to consensus for previous problems, this time, one group contends the solution is 13½, while the others believe it's 13⅓. Tracy asks two students with different solutions to draw their pictures on the board and explain them (see Figure 4.2).

"I drew nine lines," Deron says.

"And what were his nine lines representing?" Tracy asks.

"Cheese," responds another student.

"Then I took them and wrote lines [uses eraser to divide each long line into three shorter lines]," Deron continues. "And then this would be 1, 2, 3, 4, 5, 6, 7, 8, 9 [points to top nine groups of two thirds]."

"Can you circle for me what you're talking about?" Tracy requests, and Deron circles the nine groups of two thirds (Figure 4.2).

"This would be nine pizzas [points to circled groups], and then you add these four [draws swoops under four groups of two thirds and numbers them 10, 11, 12, 13], and then there's one right there [points to remaining piece]. Thirteen and one third."

"Thirteen and one half," insists Stacey, and Tracy invites her to come to the board and draw her solution beside Deron's as she explains it [see Figure 4.3].

"Can we talk about that in our groups? Some of us are saying thirteen and a half pizzas, and some of us are saying thirteen and one third," Tracy says, and after a minute, she continues, "George is going to talk to us a little bit to explain what his answer is going to be."

"Okay, it's not asking how many pieces there are," explains George. "It would be two thirds to make one pizza. We have one third left, and that can make half a pizza."

Tracy circles the number 13½, praises the group for rereading the word problem to identify that they were looking for how many pizzas they could make rather than how many pieces they had left, and continues, "I don't get what we would multiply by. Could we write this as a multiplication problem? How?"

Using the patterns that had been established in the previous division problems, Tracy's students continue to alternate between small-group and whole-class discussion to establish that, in order to divide fractions, you had to "switch the second number," to use one student's words, and multiply it by the first. This lesson ended as students generated the NSR $9/1 \times 3/2 = 27/2 = 13½$.

In the latter half of this lesson, Tracy guided her students in using specific features of visual representations to support their arguments, which is one aspect of MRC. For instance, when it was unclear how Deron's visual representation supported his argument, she asked him to clarify what he meant through circling what he was talking about. She also asked him to verbally name what the lines represented, to physically point to the components of his image that supported his argument, and to label those components, which he did by writing 10, 11, 12, and 13. In other words, Deron labeled, explained, and pointed toward specific components of his image to support his argument that the answer was 13 and ⅓ pizzas.

This aspect of MRC—using representations to support arguments or conclusions—can coincide with the comprehension strategy of visualizing as in this example in which students used visuals to support their positions. We can imagine Tracy further supporting students in visualizing by asking each group of students to hold up their visuals and identify which visuals they thought were the most helpful. For instance, in this case, a group who labeled their visual with the title, "How Many Pizzas Can Naylah Make?" might be more likely to arrive at the correct answer by focusing attention not on how many pieces were left, but on how many pizzas could be made with the pieces that were left.

FIGURE 4.3. Stacey drew this image to justify her solution to the word problem.

Similarly, students who clearly divided their bars of cheese into sections of two-thirds and labeled each section, as Tracy encouraged Deron to do, might be more likely to arrive at a correct answer than students who drew realistic pieces of cheese that were not divided into sections of two-thirds. In other words, we imagine CSI and MRC instruction in which students have opportunities to produce a variety of visuals and evaluate whether the visuals help them to reason through problems and arrive at plausible conclusions.

In addition to visualizing, rereading has long been recommended as an especially useful comprehension strategy in mathematics (Fogelberg et al., 2008), a discipline in which many texts are brief and in which each word, symbol, or number can carry information that is essential for understanding or solving problems. For instance, the same written instructions can change in meaning if the article *a* is replaced with *the*; the same image can change in meaning if its sides are labeled with different symbols; the same dot—if placed a few millimeters higher—can change from signifying a decimal point to a multiplication sign; and more. In other words, mathematics is a discipline of extreme precision, which may require students to reread their own work, their peers' work, and the original word problems to ensure that they understand the context of a given problem.

In the lesson above Tracy encouraged her students to reread by asking them to reinterpret their images after they had reread the word problem. In this type of rereading, students revisited one mode in light of the information they had learned from another. This example shows that the strategy of rereading extends across multiple modes: Students can reread a word problem after drawing an image of that problem; they can reread images after making NSRs of the images; they can reread their NSRs after using manipulatives, and so forth. In this type of rereading, students make comparisons across modes and explicitly note congruences and incongruences. Rereading, in addition to enhancing students' comprehension of the situation, also meets the second aspect of MRC by encouraging students to examine the relationships between modes more closely. Furthermore, students who reread and revisit multiple modes may meet national standards (e.g., Textbox 4.3) as they ensure that each mode precisely communicates the same solution with no deviations among them.

> **TEXTBOX 4.3**
>
> **CCSS.Math.Practice.MP6**
>
> Attend to precision.
>
> Mathematically proficient students try to communicate precisely to others.

Other Applications of MRC with Visuals

Tracy designed her instruction to help students become proficient at visualizing and rereading in mathematics in many other ways throughout the school year. She accomplished this goal through frequently asking students to produce and evaluate a variety of visuals, which they checked by rereading the original written scenarios. For instance, in a lesson on probability, students worked in small groups to discuss and illustrate possible answers to the following multiple choice question:

Justine has a bag with 12 blue marbles, 6 green marbles, 8 purple marbles, and 4 red marbles. If she wants the probability of picking a blue marble to be ½, what should Justine do?

(a) add two green, two purple, and two red marbles;
(b) add two blue marbles;

(c) remove one green, one purple, and one red marble;

(d) add six blue marbles.

Several of the group's drawings were iconic, or realistic, images such as circles in a bag. These visuals, however, did not help students envision how they could solve the problem, and they were still stuck when the time came to share their solutions. Tracy redirected the discussion by asking students to reread the problem and identify "What do you want the end result to be?," to which students responded they wanted there to be a 50% chance of drawing a blue marble. She then asked students to change their images to align more with this desired end result.

After students redid their drawings, Tracy copied Group One's illustration on the whiteboard (see Figure 4.4) and asked the students to tell her what they noticed about it. They noted that the marbles were in two groups: one of blue marbles and one of non-blue marbles; this enabled them to see more easily how many marbles they would have to add to the first group. Tracy concluded, "So what would I have to add to this group [points to blue marbles] to give me a 50% chance of drawing a blue marble?" to which a student responded "one row of six" and subsequently identified D as the answer. Tracy then asked her students to state what they liked about Group One's visual, leading to a discussion surrounding what constituted a quality visual in mathematics. This discussion resulted in a consensus that visuals should allow people to solve problems—in this case, by putting the marbles into two groups—but the picture of the marbles in the bag (or drawing something simply as it would look in real life) was not as helpful. This discussion also helped students meet the standards in Textbox 4.4 as they used a representation to interpret a scenario.

> **TEXTBOX 4.4**
>
> **NCTM Representation Standards for Grades 6–8**
>
> Instructional programs should enable all students to
>
> » create and use representations to organize, record, and communicate mathematical ideas;
> » select, apply, and translate among mathematical representations to solve problems;
> » use representations to model and interpret physical, social, and mathematical phenomena.

In addition to supporting students in visualizing, as in this example, teachers can also support their students in making and checking predictions based on patterns noted in their visuals. In the classroom example described previously, Tracy's students used the visual features of Figure 4.1 to make predictions about other numbers in the sequence. To sup-

FIGURE 4.4. Tracy and her students evaluated this image's ability to help them solve the problem.

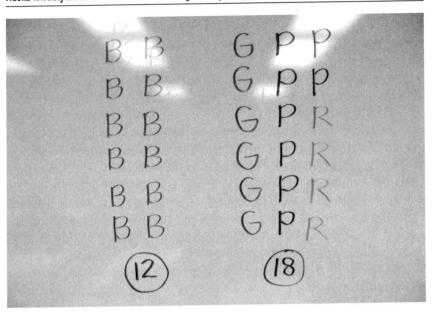

port this kind of prediction on a different kind of visual, Grace's students graphed two equations ($y = x$, $y = \frac{1}{2}x$) then predicted what would happen to the slope when the equation was changed to $y = \frac{1}{4}x$ and again to $y = \frac{1}{8}x$.

After students noted how the lines on the graph became less steep as the number in front of the x decreased, Grace said, "Now let's go in the other direction. We've been using fractions. What else could we use?" One student responded, "Whole numbers," to which Grace suggested that students go back to their calculators and type the number 2 in front of the x. "Now what do you think this line is going to look like?" she prompted, to which Jon replied, "It's going to be like the highest one. The whole number is going to be steepest," showing with his arm what he meant.

Students then checked their predictions by looking at the actual graph of the equation, a process that continued as they entered additional whole numbers in front of the x. The lesson concluded with students writing summaries of the patterns they noticed, such as, "As the number in front of the x increases, the line on the graph becomes steeper; as the number in front of the x decreases, the line on the graph becomes less steep." As a final activity, students could select additional numbers to further test this statement, including numbers they suspect might disconfirm their findings.

In this lesson students used features of the graph to make claims about the relationship between "the number in front of the *x*" and the steepness of the line. This lesson therefore supported the first aspect of MRC as students used the graph's features to make predictions and to support their claims about patterns. This lesson also featured literacy instruction as students applied the comprehension strategies of predicting and checking their predictions, as well as summarizing their findings. Thus Grace used comprehension strategies and MRC instruction to enhance students' mathematical activity as they looked at patterns in visuals and used them to draw conclusions.

One final example will illustrate how comprehension strategies can help students understand and produce a different kind of visual in mathematics: three-dimensional geometric shapes and manipulatives. Three-dimensional manipulatives, like two-dimensional drawings, enable students to visualize problems, to make predictions about solutions or patterns, and to "read across modes" by ensuring that their three-dimensional visual coheres with their numeric/symbolic one. For instance, Grace's and Tracy's students all used small cubes to form rectangular prisms, then derived the formula for the volume of rectangular prisms based on the shapes they had constructed.

In other words, they compared their individual rectangular prisms and noted that multiplying the length, width, and height of a rectangular prism always resulted in an answer that was the same number of cubes they had used to construct the prism. In this example, as in the graph example, students made predictions about a generalization (volume of a rectangular prism = width x length x height), checked their predictions through looking at their peers' rectangular prisms, and summarized the pattern they found across all rectangular prisms. As with the example of the graph, students used features of visuals to support claims, which is one aspect of MRC.

Therefore, comprehension strategies that have historically applied to written texts—such as visualizing, predicting and checking predictions, making connections, rereading, and summarizing—are not irrelevant add-ons within the discipline of mathematics. Instead, they can be central means through which students engage in mathematical reasoning as they interpret and produce a variety of visuals, connect these visuals to other modes, make predictions about solutions and patterns based on visuals, and summarize their observations. These comprehension strategies also develop multimodal representational competence as students learn how different representations relate to one another and as they use the features of these representations to justify their generalizations.

MULTIMODAL REPRESENTATIONAL COMPETENCE AND MATHEMATICAL ARGUMENTATION

Why do people use particular forms of numeric/symbolic representations, particular images, particular graphs, and particular words to make mathematical arguments? Often, these representations are not selected solely because they enable people to solve a particular problem, but because these particular representations would be the most persuasive in proving a particular (ideological) point. As Stoessiger (2002) has argued,

> When we move our interest from pure mathematics to the practical uses of mathematics in the world, the domain of numeracy, it is necessary to recognize that how we use numbers (and other mathematical ideas), why we use some particular numbers rather than others, and the language we surround them with are all value-laden, dependent on their cultural contexts, and often highly political. (p. 18)

Building MRC in mathematics can therefore include discussions of why people chose particular forms of representation to make particular arguments in real-world contexts.

The following vignette illustrates how Kurt, originally inspired by an article from *The Mathematics Teacher* (Brown & Davis, 1990), sought to foster his students' critical numeracy and build their multimodal representational competence.

> Kurt's students read the following writing prompt: The Nominating Committee for the Academy Awards has been accused of ageism in its granting of awards to women over the past several decades. They have asked you to investigate this issue and to write a report to the committee in which you confirm or deny evidence of ageism. Using data on the number of men and women who won the award since 1990, please present your findings to the nominating committee. Be sure to present your argument in the most convincing way.

Students work in pairs to decide how they will represent the problem. Several groups decide to calculate the average age of men (44 years) and women (38 years), arguing that women who win Oscars are on average 6 years younger than men. Another group makes a number line and places a pink *W* for each woman above the line (e.g., a *W* above 33 for Emma Thompson) and a blue *M* for each man below the line (e.g., an *M* below 52 for Al Pacino). This representation shows that more women are clustered in the 20s, 30s, and 40s while more men are clustered in the 30s, 40s, and 50s.

Yet another group makes a table with the labels "Men" and "Women" at the top of each column, putting a tally mark under the column of the older gender for each year. This group argues that for 17 years, the man who was granted the award was older than the woman, while women were older than men for only 6 years. A final group makes two pie charts—one showing the ages of female winners and one showing the ages of male winners—that illustrate the percentage of awardees who won at ages 20–30, ages 31–40, ages 41–50, ages 51–60, and ages 61–80.

Kurt asks the groups to share their representations with the class but adds two additional representations: a stem-and-leaf plot (Figure 4.5) and a calculation of the median age of Oscar winners: 44 for men and 33.5 for women. Kurt's students vote on which representations provide the most compelling evidence of ageism and explain why they voted in the way that they did. Students then return to their partners to write a brief report to the nominating committee using several forms of representation to justify their argument.

In this lesson, Kurt helped his students recognize that different representations can depict the same phenomenon in different ways (the fifth aspect of MRC; see "Multimodal Representational Competence Across Disciplines" in Chapter 1) depending on the goals and positions of the people making the representation. Somebody with a vested interest in protecting the Academy, for example, could point out that the three oldest Oscar winners over the past decades were women and that the average age for both men and women was "around 40." Somebody who did not need to protect the Academy, on the other hand, might emphasize that a majority of women earned awards in their 20s and 30s, while a majority of men earned their awards in their 30s and 40s.

To further reinforce the notion that our personal positions shape our mathematical arguments, Kurt could assign different roles to students

FIGURE 4.5. This stem-and-leaf plot represented the data set.

Age of Female Academy Award Winnners (1990-2012)		Age of Male Academy Award Winners (1990-2012)
	0	
	1	
9 9 8 6 5	2	9
9 9 6 5 5 4 3 3 3 2 0	3	2 2 6 7 7 8 8 9
9 5 5 2	4	0 2 3 5 5 6 7 8
	5	0 0 2 4
2 1	6	0 0
	7	
0	8	
	9	

in relation to the data set, such as a lawyer whose job was to defend the Academy against lawsuits claiming ageism, versus an aging actress who sought to prove she was denied an award because she was relatively old. Students would then have to choose or produce the representation that would most clearly bolster his or her position. Kurt could then end this lesson in a discussion about why different people might choose particular representations to frame the data. These types of discussions would support students in recognizing that mathematics is not acultural, apolitical, or acontextual, but instead is often used by people who seek to assert self-interested arguments. These types of discussions would also help students to meet national standards related to mathematical argumentation, such as the one in Textbox 4.5.

> **TEXTBOX 4.5**
>
> **CCSS.Math.Practice.MP3**
>
> Construct viable arguments and critique the reasoning of others.

Critical Numeracy in Mathematics

Critical numeracy can be applied in other ways throughout the school year as teachers and students bring in real-life mathematical texts from popular media and evaluate the arguments made within them. One of our favorite texts for teaching critical numeracy is an article titled "Which Country Has the Best Brains?" (2010). Our students have used the title to predict what, if anything, would be a fair measure to answer that question, which leads to discussions about definitions of *smart* as being relative. Students then see how the BBC answered that question—by comparing the number of Nobel Prizes each country has received since 1901.

Although the representation is clear that the United States earned more prizes than the United Kingdom, the seeming "line graph" format initially makes the data appear as though the United States' "brains" dipped below the United Kingdom's over time. Moreover, reading this text raises questions of who granted the Nobel awards and whether their decisions reflected a regional or cultural bias. By using high-interest mathematical texts such as these to discuss who produced representations, whether the representations really indicate what the authors claim they do, and how the format of the representations are themselves arguments, we contend that mathematics teachers can apprentice students into critically evaluating the mathematical claims they see in the media around them.

Tracy moved toward critical numeracy instruction in another way: by encouraging students to question how data are initially constructed and collected. In terms of national standards, the purpose of her lesson was to give students additional practice with translating fractions into percentages and to teach students about the purposes and uses of circle graphs. She began this lesson by splitting her class into seven groups, with each group surveying 25 sixth-graders of their choosing. Groups created different multiple-choice answers to the same sets of questions, such as "What is your favorite food to eat at the movies?" In other words, whereas one group listed "popcorn, licorice, pretzels, and Junior Mints" as answers, another group's answers included a different set of foods. After surveying 25 people, students converted their fractions to percentages and reported their final results as a circle graph.

Some students noted that several groups' circle graphs appeared to be different, even though they surveyed the same general population and asked the same general question. Although the lesson ended there, Tracy could have led students into a discussion of *why* the results were different, including a discussion of how the students sampled different subsections of the population and the ways in which the wording of their questions influenced their outcomes. As in Kurt's case, we could imagine Tracy assigning students different roles, such as "You are the president of a popcorn machine company [or a company that sells candy vending machines]. Using the results of your survey, make a representation arguing why the owner of a movie theatre should purchase your machine instead of another one." Students' survey instruments and circle graphs would then be constructed to prove their point, and a critical discussion afterward would center on how people can (and often do) collect and report data in ways that benefit their position.

A variety of ideologically charged statistics and poll results are frequently reported in political advertisements and the news. But some research (Rosario-Ramos, 2010) has suggested that adolescents are less likely to question quantitative arguments as opposed to linguistic arguments, even though quantitative arguments are affected by the manner in which people collect data, the instruments they use to measure a particular phenomenon, the populations from which they sample, and so forth. We believe it is important for students to recognize that quantitative claims, too, are shaped by human fallibility and opinion, and engaging them in producing and evaluating mathematical representations from different perspectives can help students achieve this critical awareness.

SUPPORTING MULTIMODAL NUMERACY THROUGH THINK-ALOUDS

Metacognition—the ability to monitor one's thought processes and adjust them to meet the demands of the situation—enhances students' mathematical reasoning (National Council of Teachers of Mathematics, 2000). There are at least two interrelated instances in which students can practice metacognition: when solving problems and when interpreting "everyday" mathematical texts. Interactive think-alouds can increase students' metacognition in these two areas. In interactive think-alouds, teachers model how a mathematician might think when faced with a text, and they structure conversations so students gain practice with "thinking like a mathematician" as well. In other words, interactive think-alouds are windows into the thought processes of an advanced practitioner. They are based on the assumption that students may not be familiar with the frameworks that a mathematician would use to solve a tough problem or interpret the quality of a graph, and consequently teachers can model for students the kinds of things they think when faced with problems or data displays.

Mathematics teachers can support students' metacognition in the domain of problem solving through modeling different approaches that mathematicians might use when faced with a challenging problem. Specifically, they can develop a plan regarding the solution, evaluate the effectiveness of this plan, recognize when it is not working, try to solve the problem in another way, and determine whether they arrived at a potentially reasonable solution.

Throughout this process, metacognitive problem-solvers use multiple comprehension strategies. For example, they may recognize that they did not quite "get" a word problem the first time and *reread* it; use common benchmark numbers (e.g., .5 for .47) to make *predictions* about the solution; *make connections* to similar but simpler problems and use them as a template for solving the current problem; *visualize* the scenario through producing a drawing or graph; *make additional connections* by comparing their visuals to their NSRs or to the original written problem; *ask questions* if there are discrepancies between the two modes; *check their initial predictions* to see if their answers seem reasonable; *make inferences* about how their solutions should be presented for greatest effect; and *summarize* to a peer how they arrived at their solutions.

In addition to using comprehension strategies to solve problems, people also often use them to interpret everyday mathematical texts. As one example of this type of interpretation, Paulos (1996) described how he used a mathematical lens while reading the news. In *A Mathematician Reads the Newspaper* he outlined how he questioned politically motivated claims presented through graphs, numbers, tables, and words. His approach could also be extended to other "everyday" popular cultural texts as students question how mathematical representations are used to support arguments regarding issues that are important to them. For instance, students can question claims regarding immigrants' impact on the economy, claims regarding whether a program at their school actually leads to higher test scores, or claims about their favorite food's effects on health.

Comprehension strategies, too, can enhance students' interpretation of popular texts. Students can *ask questions* about how data were collected and how a particular construct was measured; *make inferences* about how the text reflects the financial or political interests of the author; *make connections* between the written portion of the article and the NSRs to ascertain whether the author's take actually reflects the numeric data; produce an alternative *visualization* for the same set of data; *summarize* the author's argument and the evidence supporting that argument; and *evaluate* the quality of the author's overall conclusions.

After teachers have modeled how to conduct verbal or written think-alouds on a variety of multimodal texts, students can practice the same habits of mind, at times with prompts to guide their thinking such as these:

- What is happening in this scenario, and what is it asking me to do?
- Given what I know, what do I predict the solution of this problem will be? Did my solution match my prediction?
- Are there any patterns in the data?
- What relationships do I notice?
- Do I know of any formulas that would help me solve this problem?
- What representation could I make (e.g., table, list) that would help me visualize this problem?
- This [graph, three-dimensional model] matches this [table, visual image] because . . .
- This [form of representation] does not communicate the same information as this [form of representation] because . . .
- To improve my visual, I could . . .
- How do the authors use labels and words to frame the numeric or graphical representation in a particular way? How might other labels or words frame the issue in a different way?
- Why did the author select the intervals for this graph, and how might the graph appear different with smaller or larger intervals?
- How might the authors' methods of collecting data have affected their final claims?
- Is there another way to interpret these data other than the interpretation offered by the author?
- I still have questions about . . .

When students use and compare multiple representations while reasoning through problems, they can become more proficient mathematical thinkers. A variety of comprehension strategies, too, support students' mathematical proficiency as they interpret and critically evaluate a wide range of texts.

CHAPTER INSIGHTS

Mathematics is often associated with the numeric/symbolic mode. To be sure, interpreting NSRs, performing operations with them, and translating them to other modes are core components of representational competence in this discipline. This mode may appear to be objective and acultural because it eliminates the inclusion of "subjective" markers, such as personal pronouns (e.g., "I think"), causing many adolescents to accept numeric claims unquestioningly. Literacy instruction in mathematics therefore must also include teaching students to interrogate the seeming objectivity of this mode by questioning how mathematical claims are constructed and presented.

Despite the centrality of NSRs, other modes also play critical roles in mathematics, including written and verbal language, images, and the gestures that connect them. Students can become more proficient with these representations as they use one mode to explain another, such as using verbal speech to explain an NSR, or using a visual image to verify a numeric solution. Comprehension strategies that have traditionally helped students understand printed texts can also help them understand mathematical representations. For instance, students can *infer* which NSR would be most appropriate for a given context, they can *make connections* between graphical and numeric solutions to the same problem, and they can use patterns in visual representations to *make predictions* about possible generalizations. In this way, CSI and MRC instruction are not gratuitous additions to mathematics instruction, but instead they can bring depth, insight, clarity, and precision to students' mathematical reasoning.

CHAPTER 5

Reading and Representing in Social Studies

Social studies courses incorporate topics of study and methods of inquiry from several disciplines, such as anthropology, ethics, philosophy, psychology, and law (National Council for the Social Studies, 1994). Recent standards (NCSS, 2013), however, have highlighted four sub-disciplines in particular: civics, economics, geography, and history. According to these standards, major concepts within and across each sub-discipline should be taught with an emphasis on asking and answering substantive questions and using valid evidence from multiple sources to support arguments.

Within the discipline of civics, national standards emphasize that students should develop civic competence, or the ability to "make informed and reasoned decisions for the public good" (NCSS, 1994, p. 213) and the ability to "apply civic virtues and democratic principles in school and community settings" (NCSS, 2013, p. 33). In these settings, people hold conflicting yet deeply held convictions in relation to a range of social issues. Students can develop the skill of empathy in order to help them navigate these conflicts in humane and informed ways.

Empathy, in a disciplinary context, does not mean agreeing, condoning, or feeling emotion in regard to another's arguments or actions. Rather, it means reconstructing frames of reference—religious, economic, political, and otherwise—in relation to others, with the intention of developing substantive understandings of their positions, rather than evaluating others' ideas based only on one's own cultural position (Lévesque, 2008). Embodied representations such as role playing can foster this kind of disciplinary empathy by literally placing students in another person's position as they consider how and why he or she would think, say, feel, and react when faced with a particular situation (Daniels, 2010; Timmins, Vernon, & Kinealy, 2005). For instance, students may embody different stakeholders as they argue over a piece of legislation from each person's viewpoint.

100

In addition to emphasizing that students should be active and responsible participants in local and national communities, national civics standards also stress that students should be able to explain the roles and interrelationships between a variety of governmental and nongovernmental groups (NCSS, 2013, p. 32). Accordingly, other texts in civics describe governmental, legal, and institutional structures and procedures, such as the U.S. Constitution. However, in contemporary society, political positions are not only expressed through written documents, but also through TV news clips, Twitter feeds, public Facebook pages, and other multimedia formats, texts that also serve as fodder for discussion on civic participation.

Economics, a second major discipline that falls under the umbrella of social studies, is characterized by a distinctive set of goals and body of texts in its own right. As in civics, national standards state that one goal of economics is to enable students to make informed decisions that improve the quality of their own and others' lives (NCSS, 2013). In contrast to civics, however, this discipline focuses more closely on how individuals and societies decide to allocate resources, such as human labor, raw materials, and money, with an emphasis on how these decisions could be made in more judicious and equitable ways. As students evaluate how governmental policies and other factors affect economies and certain groups within societies, students must often interpret a variety of data displays (Suiter & Stierholz, 2011), such as tabular information, graphs, and interactive maps and infographics showing trends over time and space.

Geography standards, by contrast, require students to analyze how the distribution of landforms, water bodies, and natural resources affects human culture and activity as well as how human activity shapes physical features in return. For students to understand this interaction between human culture and environments, they must develop "spatial and environmental perspectives" (NCSS, 2013, p. 40). Spatial perspectives are about "whereness," and they involve using visual representations to make inferences about why people locate in particular regions and the consequences of their decisions. Students who have developed environmental perspectives can view human activity within the context of small- and large-scale interacting ecosystems as they make decisions that protect the environment. In addition to reading written texts and data displays, as in other disciplines, students of this discipline interpret a variety of maps, photographs of regions and people, and geospatial technologies (Fitzpatrick, 2011).

History, the fourth and final core discipline in social studies, engages students in analyzing change and continuity over time. To meet national standards in this discipline (NCSS, 2013) students must grapple with issues of causality and significance as they explore the factors that led to specific events or as they evaluate the lasting impact of actions, inventions, ideas, or movements (Brophy, 1996; Carr, 1961). For some students, history is more powerful when they can see how past and current events affect the groups with which they affiliate. In other words, adolescents who identify with particular groups (e.g., a religious or linguistic group) often feel a greater personal connection when they explore questions that address how contemporary and historical ideas and events affect "people like me" (Levstik, 2000).

Much as in the other social studies disciplines, students of history learn to interpret texts from both empathetic and critical frameworks. Specifically, "reading like a historian" entails *sourcing,* or considering a text's attribution, including the affiliations of the author/photographer/director and how the text came into being; *contextualizing,* or situating a text in time and place; *corroborating,* or confirming facts, accounts, or details across multiple sources; and *close reading,* or considering the nuances of the authors' positions and ideas and the techniques that they use to say it (Wineburg, 1991; Wineburg, Martin, & Monte-Sano, 2011). The Common Core State Standards (National Governors Association Center for Best Practices & Council of Chief State School Officers, 2010) affirm these skills when they state that readers should compare and contrast the perspectives conveyed by different sources, identify authors' purposes for producing texts, and note the rhetorical techniques by which people assert their point-of-view. Reading in this discipline often also entails evaluating which sources would be most authoritative or helpful for answering particular research questions.

Although written primary source documents are central to the work of historians (Barton, 2005), the study of history entails the interpretation of multimodal texts as well. Because humans' ideas and experiences are expressed in a myriad of ways, other objects of study in this discipline include visual and auditory sources, ranging from audio-recordings of speeches and music, to images such as photographs and political cartoons. Several people (Baron, 2012; Field, Labbo, Wilhelm, & Garrett, 1996) have also extended critical frameworks for reading written documents to physical objects, such as monuments, artifacts, or museum displays. In accordance with this view that students of social studies often interpret a wide range of modes, the following vignettes describe how several social studies teachers provided literacy instruction on multimodal texts in ways that enhanced their students' understandings of disciplinary concepts. In our analysis of each vignette, we also describe how this type of instruction fostered students' multimodal representational competence.

PHOTOGRAPHS, MAPS, GRAPHS, CARTOONS: READING IMAGES IN SOCIAL STUDIES

Images in social studies are unique because, taken collectively, they tend to be more diverse than images in other disciplines (Wilson & Landon-Hays, in press). These diverse image types include aesthetically oriented images, such as cartoons or famous works of art; naturalistic images, such as photographs or realistic drawings; and explanatory images, such as maps of trading routes or graphs of population demographics. Understanding that practitioners of social studies read a wide array of visuals, Kate sought to incorporate many different types of images into her instruction. She hoped that through this approach she could help her students feel at home with analyzing different types of visuals and using them as evidence to support claims.

The vignette below describes one lesson in which Kate's students interpreted and synthesized information from a variety of visuals. This lesson occurred during part of a larger unit on industrialization and immigration to the United States at the turn of the 20th century. Kate frequently referred to this unit as the "Push Me/Pull Me Unit" because it addressed the reasons why immigrants were "pushed" out of other countries and "pulled" into the United States. Because she taught in a city on the United States–Mexico border where many residents were immigrants, Kate also sought to draw from her students' own experiences with immigration throughout this unit.

> Kate displays a line graph and asks students to tell her what they think the graph is about. By looking at the title, students tell her that the graph is about how the number of immigrants to the United States has changed over time. They identify the numbers "on the bottom" (x-axis) are in intervals of 10 years, beginning in 1830 and ending in 2000, while the numbers "on the side" (y-axis) are in intervals of one million, representing the number of immigrants that arrived in the United States at a given time.

After making these general observations, students work in pairs to annotate the graph by writing observations, questions, and inferences in accordance with the guiding questions that Kate had given them. After students had interpreted and discussed the graph in pairs, Kate begins a whole-class discussion: "What are some things you noticed about this graph?"

"The line is highest in 1910 and 2000."

"The line graph peaks in 1910 and 2000. What does that mean?"

"More immigrants came to the United States in those years than in other years."

"Right. Did you have any guesses for why you think that is?"

"In 2000, a lot of people came from Mexico because they wanted a better life in the United States."

"They wanted better jobs or their kids to get a better education than they got in Mexico."

"That's probably why people came in 1910 too."

"So they wanted a better life in the United States," Kate rejoins. "And immigrants came for the same reasons in 1910 that they come today?"

"Maybe they wanted more jobs. Like they could get work in the factories."

"Or maybe there was something bad in their own countries."

"With industrialization in the United States, immigrants could get jobs working in places like factories, and maybe they felt life here would be better than life in their home countries," Kate summarizes. "Why do you think more immigrants came in those particular decades than in other decades?"

Students continue to discuss the line graph, including making further predictions regarding why immigration might have been higher in some eras and lower in others, or why more immigrants might have come from some areas of the world but not from others.

In this vignette, Kate fostered representational competence while providing comprehension instruction on a line graph. She required her students to use specific features of a representation to support their predictions about why people immigrated during particular decades. She also taught students to attend to text features, such as headings and labeled intervals, and use them to summarize the main idea of the text, which is another comprehension-building practice of successful readers (Duke & Pearson, 2002).

Kate continues: "Do you think in the 1910s, people were coming from Mexico or Latin America like in the 2000s?"

When students do not predict where immigrants would be coming from in the 1910s, Kate projects two visuals on the board. The first is a pie chart titled "Immigration to the United States: Where They Came From: 1880–1920." This pie chart shows which percentage of immigrants came from "Northwestern Europe," "Eastern and Southern Europe," and "the Rest of the World."

The second visual is a map titled "Immigration to the United States: 1880–1920." This map contains arrows from different countries to the United States. Thicker arrows represent larger populations of immigrants, and thinner arrows represent smaller populations. For instance, the arrow from Italy to the United States is the thickest line, indicating that more immigrants came from this country than from other countries, and this arrow is labeled with the number 4,114,103.

"By looking at these visuals," Kate prompts, "Can you tell me now where most of the immigrants came from in the 1910s?"

Students say that in 1910 most immigrants came from "Eastern and Southern Europe," according to the label on the pie chart. They then use the specific labels on the map to clarify that many immigrants from "Southern Europe" came from Italy and many immigrants from "Eastern Europe" came from Russia. They also note that, although the pie chart simply says "Rest of the World," this label must have included Japan and China, whose immigration statistics were represented on the map. Students note that the thinner arrows from China and Japan lead to California, whereas the thicker arrows from European countries lead to New York.

Finally, students read a brief informational text describing "push me/pull me" factors that encouraged immigrants to come to the United States during this time period, and they share how their own family's motivations for immigrating compared to those of immigrants from the early 20th century.

In this vignette, Kate fostered another aspect of her students' MRC by asking them to explain the relationship between the pie chart and the map. Students described how labels on the pie chart, such as "Rest of the World," correlated with labels on the map, such as the arrows labeled "China" and "Japan."

This component of MRC correlates with the comprehension strategy of making connections, when students compare two authors' methods of framing or labeling the same issue. In this case further discussion might have focused on similarities and differences between the labels on the map and the pie chart, including questioning why the authors chose different labels for the same phenomenon. For instance, students might question why the author of the pie chart framed immigration in terms of Europe and "the Rest of the World," rather than mentioning Asian

> **TEXTBOX 5.1**
>
> **CCSS.ELA-Literacy. RH.6-8.6**
>
> Identify aspects of a text that reveal an author's point of view or purpose (e.g., loaded language, inclusion or avoidance of particular facts).

countries by name as the author of the map did. This side-by-side comparison of the authors grouped the data that would perhaps reveal how one author's description was more Eurocentric than the other's, and would help students to meet national standards related to critical literacy in social studies (e.g., Textbox 5.1).

To further foster her students' ability to interpret, critique, and produce representations, Kate could have asked her students to identify which representation was more helpful in answering their question, or which one(s) they would have used if the U.S. government had asked them to compile a report on immigration statistics from that era. The ensuing discussion would allow students to use the features and affordances of each representation (e.g., the specificity of the map) to justify which representation they liked better.

In order to further develop her students' representational competence in social studies Kate could have asked them, "How would you improve this representation?" Kate's students could have critiqued the pie chart by creating a new pie chart that named Japan and China or created an improved map that showed percentages instead of raw numbers. In the next vignette Kate continued to incorporate visuals into her lesson.

Kate introduces a new assignment to her students: they will write a series of brief journal entries as though they were immigrants to the United States after 1890—a date they had learned signified a "new" type of immigrant, one who was escaping for economic, political, or social reasons and was drawn to life in the city. In this journal they will do the following:

- Identify the country from which they came
- Explain why their characters left their homeland
- Describe their characters' journey and arrival to the United States

- Describe living and working conditions in the United States during this time
- Explain whether the immigrant chose to "Americanize" (or not) and why
- Speculate on what the future held for their character

To scaffold students in completing this assignment, Kate gives them a paper with photographs on the left side and space for writing on the right side. The photographs sequentially feature immigrants on a ship to the United States, followed by immigrants being inspected at Ellis Island, and finally images of "ethnic enclaves" and tenements that illustrated the crowded living conditions in which many immigrants lived. For each image, students answer the questions: What do I see? (evidence); What do I think? (interpretation of the evidence); and Why do I think this? (evidence and interpretation linked together).

One of the first photographs is the image in Figure 5.1. When discussing, "What do I think," Miguel asserts that some people on the boat "look rich and others look poor." Kate asks, "What information from the photograph proves your thinking?" to which Miguel responds by pointing to a man in a hat and jacket who appears rich to him, while a woman in a shawl appears poor.

Andy asks, "Why would rich people want to leave if life was good in their own country?" and Lara interjects, "Was there all color of immigrants?" In response, Kate directs them to look at the pictures again and to consider what they had learned earlier from the maps, pie chart, and brief informational text.

Based on their recollection of the earlier pie chart, students decide that most immigrants to New York at this time were from Europe, which is why most of them appeared White. They also tentatively conclude, based on a line from the reading that mentioned first- and second-class passengers, that there was economic variation among immigrants, yet most of them were probably fairly poor because they could only pay for the cheapest form of passage on the ship.

The continued discussion and accompanying photographs inspire Lara to describe her journey as an immigrant in the following terms: "I am not very rich. I am middle class. I am 14 years old. I am going across the Atlantic Ocean. It is uncomfortable. We are crammed together. There is not much space where the poorest are. I try to make friends. The process of going to Ellis Island was long and exhausting. The journey was

FIGURE 5.1. Kate's students evaluated famous photographs of immigrants at the turn of the century. (Photo: Emigrants Coming to the "Land of Promise," Library of Congress. Retrieved from http://www.loc.gov/pictures/resource/cph.3a09957/)

uncomfortable. I was tired. The beds were hard. We were squished with people I never met or barely knew."

In this example Kate furthered her students' ability to interpret and synthesize information from multiple representations, which is one aspect of MRC (see "Multimodal Representational Competence Across Disciplines" in Chapter 1) as well as a hallmark of disciplinary reasoning. As before, students used specific features of representations to support their claims (cf. Textbox 5.2). In this case, students referred to specific subcomponents of images, such as the historical figures' clothes and their skin color, to support their tentative conclusions that immigrants to New York in the early 1900s came from varied economic backgrounds and that they were primarily White. As before, students applied the comprehension strategy of making connections by comparing information presented in these photographs to information presented in another visual (pie chart) in order to corroborate their earlier assumption that most immigrants to New York at the time appeared to be White. These types of connections also gave them practice in synthesizing visual and written information, as recommended by national standards (e.g., Textbox 5.3).

> **TEXTBOX 5.2**
>
> **CCSS.ELA-Literacy.**
> **RH.6-8.1**
>
> Cite specific textual evidence to support analysis of primary & secondary sources.

> **TEXTBOX 5.3**
>
> **CCSS.ELA-Literacy.**
> **RH.6-8.1**
>
> Integrate visual information (e.g. in charts, graphs, photographs, videos or maps) with other information in print and visual texts.

In addition to making connections to other visuals and making inferences about the photographs, Kate's students applied another comprehension strategy: asking questions, such as the question about immigrants' skin color and about why wealthy people would be motivated to leave their home countries.

To further extend this comprehension strategy, Kate could also model for her students how to ask critical questions about evidence, such as "Does this source (or set of sources) constitute sufficient evidence for making this claim, and if not, what other sources should I consult?" This type of evidence-based reasoning would have been appropriate in the vignette above when one student asked if the immigrants had different skin colors. Kate could have asked students if the photographs they had viewed were sufficient evidence for answering that question, and why or why not, then prompted students to identify additional sources they could have consulted to answer that question. In this case, students might have identified that the pie chart, which showed that most immigrants came from Europe, would have provided them with a fairly reasonable basis for assuming that many immigrants were White. (Discussions of what makes someone "White," and discussions of whether large populations "of Color" existed in Europe at that time would also have been interesting lines of inquiry.)

Questioning evidence, in addition to building historiography skills, would also build students' multimodal representational competence. Another aspect of MRC entails evaluating multimodal representations and explaining why one representation is more apt for a particular purpose than another representation. Pie charts report percentages in relation to wholes, such as the whole body of people that immigrated, whereas the photographs only depicted several dozen immigrants out of millions. Consequently, the pie chart—due to its structure and function—was probably a more useful representation for determining whether most immigrants to New York during that period could be considered White. The photographs, by contrast, were a more useful representation for validating Lara's narrative account of one immigrant's uncomfortable, cramped journey to Ellis Island. We argue that, as suggested by this example, students can explicitly discuss what types of representations would be most helpful and appropriate for their particular purposes as they seek to answer questions, construct accounts, or prove claims.

Other Examples of MRC with Visuals

The above vignettes illustrated how Kate supported her students' comprehension of a variety of visuals, including line graphs, pie charts, maps, and photographs. However, other images in social studies have more aesthetic orientations, such as cartoons or works of art. Annette's sixth-grade students frequently worked with these latter types of images, using analytic approaches similar to Kate's. For instance, much as Kate's students used specific evidence within photographs to justify inferences, Annette's students completed charts with three columns: "What do I see?" "What does the visual symbolize?" and "What does the visual mean?" As one example, students read a political cartoon titled "The Attack," which depicted two legs standing in the place of the Twin Towers on 9/11 amidst rising smoke. The caption on the bottom of the political cartoon read "Still Standing."

To respond to the question in the first column, one student stated that what she saw was "a huge man with striped pants standing where the Twin Towers fell," whereas another shared that what he saw was "Uncle Sam standing in smoke with his hand in a fist." While discussing the second column, several students confirmed that Uncle Sam with his fists clenched symbolized that the United States was angry, and discussion of the third column led another student to conclude that, "They [al Qaeda] wanted to put us in a position where we would be really weak . . . but America is still standing. We're not happy about it, but we are still standing." Annette's instruction shared commonalities with Kate's in the sense that students used specific components of images as a basis for forming inferences and predictions, which is one aspect of MRC as well as one practice of engaged readers.

In addition to forming evidence-based interpretations of various types of images, MRC also includes providing students with opportunities to produce and/or select and combine visuals of their own. Alice sought to develop this aspect of MRC in an economics lesson whose purpose was to compare and contrast the allocation of resources among various groups of people around the world. Students researched people from two different socioeconomic and geographic groups of their choosing (e.g., middle-class residents in Britain; factory workers in Indonesia). Each student then wrote a few journal entries from the perspective of each person, including tracking how much money they spent, and on what.

As students evaluated model journals, they noted which features they liked, such as a table that kept track of expenses, photographs (printed from the Internet) that showed the houses in which each person lived, photographs showing items they purchased, a map showing their neighborhood or community, a first-person narrative, so forth. Students then produced their own journals and shared, evaluated, and discussed them in small groups. This example illustrates but one type of assignment in which students of social studies can produce a multimodal text, explain why they chose the representations they did, and evaluate the effectiveness and clarity of their overall message, including making suggestions to each other regarding additional representations they might choose to illustrate a particular point.

EMBODIED REPRESENTATION IN SOCIAL STUDIES

Empathy is a key practice of thinking like a historian as students learn to evaluate people's actions, motivations, and beliefs according to others' cultural and historical frameworks, rather than according to students' own personal values (Lévesque, 2008; Yilmaz, 2007). Compassionate and informed civic engagement likewise often requires students to consider issues from others' perspectives without immediately dismissing their ideas. For instance, students can learn to consider issues from the perspective of a minority group, even if they are part of the majority, or they can genuinely consider an issue from the perspective of somebody with a different religious or political ideology.

Whereas some scholars (Foster, 2001) emphasize that this form of perspective-taking is primarily a rigorous cognitive exercise, others (Boal, 2006; Schneider, Crumpler, & Rogers, 2006) have asserted that it can also be a profoundly emotional exercise. That is, if students will be moved to take social action on behalf of another, they may have to develop affective understandings of the physical, emotional, and personal toll that certain conditions, policies, or beliefs impose upon others. Kate sought to develop this type of affective empathy as students were learning about industrialization and the rise of unions. The following vignette describes how she introduced her students to factory conditions at the turn of the 20th century.

> The room is considerably warm as students enter Kate's classroom. An orange glow radiates from space heaters strategically placed in the center of the room. Students are surprised to discover their assigned seats have been displaced. Instead they find three groups of 10 desks, each with the name of a different manufacturing company above it. Each group of desks represents an assembly line, while a CD player in the background blasts annoying, repetitive, prerecorded beating sounds.
>
> Each row of seats displays two boxes containing a Mr. Potato Head© and parts for assembly, along with an image of a highlighted Mr. Potato Head positioned in a particular stance, with specific facial expressions, and a clipboard of instructions reserved for the foreman. Kate explains their task is to correctly assemble as many Mr. Potato Heads as possible within a 20-minute timeframe and that completed products must display the arms, eyes, ears, shoes, a nose, a hat, a mouth, and a moustache in the exact position displayed in the image attached to the foreman's clipboard. Each student is responsible for placing only one specific piece repetitively into a plastic potato as it passes by them. Foremen also act as quality control agents by rejecting imperfect replications and by tallying the number of acceptable products. The timer begins the flurry of activity as each team races to complete as many perfect products as possible. The students' excitement wanes, and their moods noticeably change from spirited and carefree to aggressive and driven.

In a discussion after the activity, Kate's students report that the working conditions, as well as the competitiveness between the three assembly lines, increased levels of "frustration," "stress," and "responsibility." Several students compare themselves to "elves" as they comment on how difficult the experience must have been for people who actually worked in factories under difficult conditions. Kate then asks her students to read and annotate excerpts from "Life in the Shop" (Lemlich, 1909), a firsthand account of one woman's experiences as a shirtwaist maker, including photographs of working conditions. In their individual annotations and in a later whole-class discussion, students note similarities and differences between their experiences on the assembly line and Lemlich's experiences as communicated through the photographs and writing.

In previous vignettes, Kate used images as a way to activate students' background knowledge and to build their interest before reading primary source documents, but in this case she used an embodied representation for the same purpose. Specifically, the factory demonstration served as a transition into readings on working conditions for many women in the late 19th and early 20th century. In some ways, this lesson fostered multimodal representational competence as students explicitly compared and contrasted the content of one mode (the embodied representation) to the content of other modes (the photographs and the readings) by noting what they shared in common and by noting how they were different.

Students noted, for instance, that all sources described the task as repetitive and the consequences for failing to produce a correct product caused stress. In the classroom factory, students worked for only 20 minutes, but still experienced strong emotional reactions, whereas in the 1900s factory, women worked for 13 hours on tasks that required finer manual dexterity and more intense focus on smaller objects, leading to even greater eyestrain and other forms of physical hardship. We argue that this comparison between modes built students' empathy for the content expressed in the second mode. That is, by reflecting on how they felt physically and emotionally throughout the embodied representation, they recognized how much harder it would have been for people working under even worse conditions for more extended durations of time.

In addition to building students' multimodal representational competence by requiring them to compare and contrast the information presented across multiple modes, this lesson also supported students' comprehension. By annotating the written passage and discussing their annotations, students were able to clarify their understandings of both the passage and the preceding embodied representation. Although Kate did not provide any additional instruction on what should be in the annotation in this particular lesson, throughout the year she had established a classroom environment that emphasized the importance of "talking to the text" through writing inferences, predictions, summaries, questions, or connections in the margins of the historical documents that they read.

After this demonstration, students looked at notecards that Kate provided, each of which included sentence starters related to comprehension strategies, and used them to ask additional questions about working conditions or words they did not understand, to make inferences about why workers endured these conditions or why women were selected to work at these factories instead of men, to predict how this experience influenced many women who had not previously worked outside of the home, and to summarize what they had learned from the embodied experience as well as from the primary source document.

Other Applications of MRC with Embodied Representations

Alice likewise often used embodied representations to engage her students in social studies concepts. In one lesson, for instance, her students viewed maps and simple tables that showed tariff rates on common imports. They then walked around the room, with each person representing a country, as they exchanged cards representing goods. When countries had to pay higher tax rates to import products, some students debated whether or not they still wanted to buy that product from that country or whether they could acquire the same product more cheaply from another country with which the United States had a free trade agreement. These decisions resulted in a discussion after the simulation in which students speculated on why the United States established tariffs, and on how international businesses could still find ways to sell their goods at competitive prices, even when people might have to pay an additional tax on their product.

In another lesson, Alice's students read about different types of government and then worked in groups to produce skits representing each type. In one skit a member of the group sat up high on a table while people below her begged for their interests to be considered, which she did not always do before making proclamations. One class member guessed that this skit represented an autocracy after noting that "one person makes decisions for others who don't get a vote." At the end of this activity, students reflected on the disadvantages and advantages of different forms of government and identified the ones under which they would most like to live based on the skits as well as their readings.

In both examples from Alice's classroom, students practiced aspects of multimodal representational competence by transforming what they learned through one mode (tables, maps, writing) into an embodied representation and by reflecting on what they learned from both modes. These examples share commonalities with Kate's previous example in the sense that embodied representations provided students with an insider's perspective on the targeted disciplinary concept. The student who represented businesses in China, for instance, had to consider how she could still provide toys at competitive prices to the United States despite tariffs, whereas the pleading students enacted the frustration that people would feel if their perspectives were not considered when their leaders made decisions concerning them.

For this reason, we argue that embodied representations align with the disciplinary goal of conducting empathetic readings, in which students understand a phenomenon from different insiders' perspectives (e.g., understand the rise of labor unions from the perspective of a union worker), and analytical readings, in which students consider the causes and effects of particular phenomena (e.g., consider the effects of tariffs on businesspeople). Much as with printed texts, these interpretations or productions of embodied texts can be enhanced through the use of comprehension strategies, as specified in the following examples:

- Stopping the embodied representations and *making predictions* about what historical actors would do next in the given situation, such as how the factory workers would respond to difficult conditions and why they would respond that way; or how businesspeople in particular countries would respond to high tariffs.
- *Checking predictions* through reading other texts to discover the actual choices that historical actors made and why they made those choices.
- *Making connections* between modes by noting how conditions or events presented in one mode (e.g., embodied representation) compare and contrast to those presented in another mode (e.g., writing).
- *Summarizing the content* of the embodied representation, such as summarizing the differences between types of government in

the skits. Alternatively, summarizing can entail using embodied representations to summarize what was learned from another source, such as when students summarized the meaning of "autocracy" through acting it out.

- *Making inferences* about the motives and reasons behind historical figures' decisions based on students' embodiment of those figures, such as one student's observation that the factory owners seemed to be motivated by money rather than by any moral concerns for their workers.
- *Asking questions,* including asking questions about causality, significance, ethics, or other concerns related to civic and historical habits of mind, such as questions regarding whether laws were needed to stop the factory owners' harmful practices or whether they would behave ethically without laws.

Embodied representations hold the potential to enhance students' empathetic engagement with disciplinary concepts in social studies. Embodied representations may also build students' representational competence as they compare and contrast these representations with others, and as they use embodied media to synthesize and consolidate their understandings of disciplinary concepts. As with printed texts, comprehension strategies can deepen students' understandings of these embodied texts as well.

MULTIMODAL REPRESENTATIONAL COMPETENCE AND ARGUMENTATION

Argumentation is central to the practice of economists, geographers, historians, and political scientists alike, all of whom collect or use data as evidence to support claims, evaluate the trustworthiness and significance of individual pieces of evidence or particular bodies of evidence, explain how their evidence sufficiently supports their claims, and account for disconfirming evidence or competing interpretations of the same evidence. Often, this evidence is multimodal as disciplinary practitioners synthesize information from maps, graphs, photographs, oral testimonies, and/or written accounts to support their positions.

Milly, who taught both language arts and social studies, sought to engage her students in producing reasoned and informed multimodal arguments in a unit whose essential question was: In what ways, and to what extent, should the U.S. federal government be involved in protecting the rights and promoting the quality of life for American citizens? Near the end of the unit, Milly gave her students several writing prompts that required them to articulate their own opinions on this topic, as well as to take the perspective of prominent politicians. The vignette below describes how Milly supported students in responding to one of the writing prompts.

Writing prompt: Since the U.S. federal government was created, people have debated the role that the federal government should play in the lives of American citizens, including its role in the following areas:

- Public education
- Health care
- Protecting the environment
- Defining and protecting people's civil rights
- Regulating food and drugs
- Providing social security for the elderly
- Providing assistance for the poor or unemployed
- Establishing a national bank
- Building a national infrastructure for transportation

You have selected a contemporary or historical political figure whose opinions address the following question: In what ways, and to what extent, should the federal government be involved in protecting the rights and promoting the quality of life for American citizens? Please research your figure's opinions in relation to *one* of the domains listed above; then please use the paper provided to make a Facebook page for your political figure in which you include at least the following:

1. A profile picture or symbolic icon that represents a key belief or characteristic of your figure.
2. Basic information, including three top identifiers for which this person is known.
3. A list of friends taken from other contemporary and historical figures in the class and beyond.
4. Three status updates in which you state major claims of yours that are relevant to the debate about the role that the national government should play in the lives of its citizens. Underneath each claim, please include one piece of evidence (e.g., a graph, a statistic, a drawing) that supports your claim.

To help her students in responding to this writing prompt, Milly gives each student a list of historical and contemporary political figures from which they can choose—such as Hillary Clinton and Alexander Hamilton—as well as suggested topics for each person, such as "establishing a national bank" for Hamilton.

Near the end of class one day, Milly's students begin a discussion on how they will go about searching for valid information on their selected topic. One student says he wants to address the role that the federal government should play in health care, so Milly decides to use this topic as the basis for modeling the search process. Milly asks students to identify promising search terms for looking up valid information in relation to this topic. After trial and error with different search terms, the students decide to select "impact of the Affordable Care Act" as a reasonable search term that will give them information on the possible effects of the federal government's intervention in regulating health care for U.S. citizens.

The following day, Milly brings paper strips of the top ten results that appeared on the search page when she typed the students' suggested term into a search engine. Working in groups of three, students rank those search results by physically placing them in order of most to least useful in terms of helping them respond to the writing prompt, and the class as a whole discusses why they ranked the search results as they did.

One group, for instance, infers that a site whose identifying line is, "Obama committed fraud to sell health-care law," presents a more conservative perspective on the law, and although they might still read the web page, they would need to find other sources by somebody with an opposing political view to verify the information. Another website, "Affordable Health Insurance Is Here: Stimulus Cash—Limited Time Offer!" is dismissed as entirely unreliable due to its overly enthusiastic intent to sell a product. A final discussion centers on whether healthcare.gov—a site run by the U.S. government—is an objective source or whether it would present an unduly positive view of the projected impact of the Affordable Care Act (ACA) on individuals' health insurance.

Still working in groups of three, each group member reads the first few pages of a different website that the class had ranked highly in their evaluation of the search results list. They note which arguments and data are the same across all three websites, as well as which arguments only appear in one source. As a whole class, they discuss what they learned from this search, as well as what their next search strategies and terms should be. After discussion, the class identifies that a possible next search term would be "impact of Affordable Care Act, Congressional Budget Office," a term that would help them identify the overall projected economic impact of the ACA as determined by the nonpartisan organization. They also identify that future helpful searches could relate to the personal and economic impacts of more centralized health care in other countries.

At the end of the lesson, students use a similar search process to find a set of useful sources that would help them gather trustworthy information about their own self-selected topic as indicated in the writing prompt.

In this lesson Milly modeled for students how to search for reliable information and how to corroborate information across multimodal websites, each of which contained a variety of Health Care Infographics, line graphs, and maps. Milly's students began the process of "evaluating the claims made in these multimodal representations," which is one aspect of MRC, by discussing which websites they thought would be

> **TEXTBOX 5.4**
>
> **CCSS.ELA-Literacy. WHST.6-8.8**
>
> Gather relevant information from multiple print and digital sources, using search terms effectively; assess the credibility and accuracy of each source.

most useful and trustworthy. Milly accomplished this task by leading discussions in which students noted whether the founders of each website exhibited a particular bias and whether or not the same claims and supporting evidence were corroborated across multiple independent sources (cf. Textbox 5.4).

As illustrated by this example, corroboration in social studies can correlate with the comprehension strategy of making connections, which in this case entailed comparing and contrasting the information in sources published by people who affiliated with different political parties. Milly's students made these connections by noting which claims were included within multiple sources and which claims were only verified by one source. As part of helping students make these connections, Milly also helped students establish *benchmark sources*, or sources to which students could assign more credence and weight, and against which they could compare other sources. For instance, Milly's first discussion concluded with the premise that statistics published by the nonpartisan Congressional Budget Office might be a reliable benchmark against which they could evaluate claims made by other, more partisan organizations if they were searching for statistics on the projected economic impact of the ACA.

In this lesson, students also applied the comprehension strategy of evaluating texts by noting the overall manner in which the multimodal websites were framed. For instance, based on their reading of the search results page, students noted that some sources framed the Affordable Care Act as a "fraud" while others framed it in terms of "security for families." By noting the overall terms used to describe the act, students identified each source's position, which enabled them to (1) purposefully select websites from both sides of the political aisle; (2) select websites with more objective terminology; and/or (3) select websites that weighed pros and cons of the ACA before making a final claim about its benefits.

After students gathered reliable information about their topics, Milly turns their attention toward the process of making their own paper Facebook pages in which they present claims about the role of the federal government through their own status updates. Milly begins the lesson by showing model Facebook pages of prominent politicians, asking students to infer what they conveyed as important to them through their choice of images. Michelle Obama's page, for instance, depicts her smiling while sitting by her children, whereas Arnold Schwarzenegger's page depicts him with his shirt off and arms upraised in a ring surrounded by adoring fans.

After identifying what each political figure wants to be known for (or at least what their strategists want them to be known for), students are encouraged to draw or find images that they believe their political figure would use as their profile picture and cover image. The student who selected Thomas Jefferson, for instance, draws a profile picture of him leaning over a desk with a quill pen writing the Declaration of Independence, while his cover picture is of his most treasured possession: his library. The student who chose Alexander Hamilton, by contrast, draws a cover photo of a 10-dollar bill overlain with an image of a building labeled "Bank of the United States."

Before making their own status updates, students also view and discuss models of other politicians who have made claims and supported them through infographics and photographs, such as Barack Obama's claim that "It's time for Congress to take action to end gun violence." Underneath this assertion, a photograph of hands scattering roses into a river is overlain with the statement: "FACT: Since 1968, more than 1.3 million Americans have died from gun violence. That's more than in all of the wars in American history *combined.*" After viewing this example and others—which illustrate how conservative and liberal politicians used photographs, statistics, and graphs to support claims in their Facebook status updates—students do the same with their own paper Facebook pages by making assertions related to what they believe the role of the federal government should be in particular domains, and supporting each assertion with a graph, photograph, infographic, or statement.

Students tape their paper Facebook pages on the walls of their classroom and walk around the class commenting on their peers' pages using sticky notes while remaining "in character," agreeing with each other's comments or writing counterclaims or disconfirming evidence underneath each status update based on the position of their character. For instance, conservative congressman Ron Paul disagrees with Hamilton's claim that a national bank should be established, based on the belief that the government should not assume any powers not specifically named in the Constitution. Barack Obama counters the news article shared by Sarah Palin, which describes individual employers who cut their employees' hours to avoid having to provide them health benefits under the ACA, by sharing a line graph that shows how average working hours have gone up in most industries since its passage.

In Milly's words, the activity "takes on a life of its own" as students continue to post on the paper Facebook pages beyond what is required of the assignment, coming up with additional postings and hashtags, such as Hamilton's "Meeting up with Aaron Burr today! #highnoon." Students then use the information in Facebook pages, including their peers' rebuttals, to write a speech to the Senate, still in character, in which they argue what the federal government's role should be in relation to one social issue.

In today's digital age, public debate, dissent, and persuasion are often multimodal. Politicians, lobbyists, news reporters, and public citizens now turn to Twitter, Facebook, YouTube videos, blogs, websites, or other social platforms in order to influence local and national conversations. This lesson provided students with a segue into this type of public forum as students used Facebook page templates to state claims, provide supporting evidence, and counter others' arguments within a social, multimodal setting. In addition to supporting national standards regarding supporting claims with evidence (cf. Textbox 5.5) this lesson also

> **TEXTBOX 5.5**
>
> **CCSS.ELA-Literacy. WHST.6-8.1b**
>
> Support claim(s) with logical reasoning and relevant, accurate data and evidence that demonstrate an understanding of the topic or text, using credible sources.

fostered multimodal representational competence by giving students practice with selecting, combining, and/or producing standard and non-standard representations. Some students, for instance, selected existing representations (e.g., a copy of the White House's published line graph on job statistics) for their pages, while others created nontraditional types of representation (e.g., images overlaid with statistics) to persuade people to adopt their arguments.

To further support students' argumentation, this lesson could have been extended by the evaluation of individual claims as students compared evidence and counterevidence underneath each status update. For instance, students could have considered the links to individual stories of people whose working hours had been reduced due to the ACA, including photographs of despondent parents, as compared to the line graph that showed that most people's working hours have increased since its passage; then they could have decided which piece of evidence carried the most weight and why. This type of analysis would have supported the comprehension strategy of evaluating by apprenticing students into developing discipline-specific frameworks for weighing evidence.

In addition to increasing students' MRC, components of this lesson also fostered students' comprehension and critical analysis of multimodal texts. Milly's students applied the comprehension strategy of inferring when they viewed model profile pictures and made conjectures about the values and identities people intended to convey. Students inferred, for instance, that people often portrayed themselves as being patriotic through color: if not through an American flag, then through other objects that were red, white, and blue. They also made inferences about gender differences as they noted that the cover pictures of many prominent women portrayed them with children or families, whereas men were more likely to be alone.

To extend inferring as a comprehension strategy, this activity could include further discussion on why politicians chose particular representations to accompany evidence for claims. For instance, students could have made inferences about why Barack Obama's team chose hands scattering flowers to accompany the statistic on gun violence, when they might have chosen among a variety of infographics (e.g., circles whose sizes were scaled to represent the relative proportion of people who died in each war; interactive maps showing the amount of gun violence in each state since 1965) to visually prove the same point.

The examples above show that argumentation in social studies is often multimodal, inasmuch as people use interactive maps, graphs, and other forms of representation to explain their rationales, prove their claims, and persuade others to adopt a particular stance. Accordingly, instruction in argumentation can include weighing different types of multimodal evidence and evaluating whether this evidence is credible and sufficient for proving claims. This instruction can also include making inferences regarding why people chose particular forms of representation—colors, graphics, photographs, or other forms of persuasion—to communicate with their constituents. Finally, students can learn to enter these dialogues themselves by coordinating different types of representation while asserting their own arguments.

Critical Literacy in Social Studies

Evaluating arguments is one component of critical literacy in this discipline as students learn to sift through and weigh varying and contradictory claims and evidence. Another component of critical literacy includes questioning implicit messages and norms, both past and present. Milly's instruction moved toward this type of critical literacy in the Facebook lesson when her students began to notice gender norms implicit in the political figures' Facebook images. As another example, Milly sought to help her students unpack implicit messages in a different lesson when her class analyzed CNN and FOX News' reports of Saddam Hussein's capture, including disheveled pictures of him subserviently opening his mouth so a doctor could inspect his teeth. Accompanying headlines proclaimed that he was "caught like a rat in a spiderhole," while another article claimed he "snarled" during his trial. Her students noted that the American media outlets' choice of words and images were designed to make him seem like an animal rather than a human being, and they assumed that the images were meant to discredit him in the eyes of his people in Iraq.

In both this lesson and the previous one, Milly used texts that were similar in form and content to the texts that students encountered in the world around them on an everyday basis: Google search engine results, Facebook pages, and multimedia reports from contemporary news media sources. Following Luke, O'Brien, and Comber (1994), we believe that *everyday texts*—defined as the texts from students' local or online communities—serve as especially potent or generative starting points for critical literacy instruction because they enable students to recognize and critique implicit norms and messages in the world around them, and not just in texts of the "past."

Often, these types of critical analysis in social studies include identifying how power operates at personal, local, national, and international levels (Soares & Wood, 2010). Social groups—including the ones to which students belong—have been shaped by political, economic, institutional, historical, and other sociocultural factors, which have led to inequity and injustice for many. Recognizing, discussing, and disrupting these forms of injustice can also therefore be a central component of social studies education.

Alice sought to develop this sense of critical awareness by giving students brief case studies that traced the production of finished products, beginning with where raw materials were grown or harvested, where they were transformed into manufactured goods, and finally where they were sold at distribution centers. On a PowerPoint slide show, she included several photographs of the conditions and goods at each stage of the production process. Students traced, for instance, how diamonds from South African mines ended up in Tiffany's jewelry stores, and how fabrics are sewn into clothes at maquiladoras on the United States–Mexico border, where young women face unhealthy and sexist working conditions for low wages. These case studies and striking photographs served as springboards for discussion as students witnessed how the people who harvested and manufactured products often worked in dangerous places for little money in less developed countries in order to benefit the more affluent people, often in more developed countries, who ultimately purchased these products.

One final purpose of critical literacy in social studies is making informed and empathetic decisions that benefit the community, or otherwise taking actions that move toward a more just society. In Alice's classroom students discussed how they might spend their money on products that did not exploit others; in other classes, critical literacy can entail taking action in other forms. Whether students attend and express opinions at local city council meetings, or commit to carpooling when possible after they learn about the impact of pollution on the environment, or organize Facebook pages on behalf of a social cause, or volunteer their time to a local organization of their choosing—one end goal of social studies education is to foster civic mindedness in which students are aware of problems in their communities and world, and in which they are motivated to take action toward improving those problems.

SUPPORTING HISTORICAL THINKING ON MULTIMODAL TEXTS THROUGH THINK-ALOUDS

Students can be apprenticed into reading by learning how skilled readers approach texts and by having multiple opportunities to practice similar approaches themselves (Schoenbach et al., 2012). This task is often accomplished in part through think-alouds, as practiced readers model their thought processes for novices while reading texts. In effect, the rationale behind think-alouds is to make invisible thought processes visible to students so that they can practice using similar thought processes.

In traditional think-alouds on printed texts, teachers often project an excerpt from a text on an interactive whiteboard and annotate it as they think aloud through asking clarification questions, making inferences, and verbally articulating other comprehension strategies. As part of the process of a think-aloud, teachers also evaluate texts according to discipline-specific concerns: In the case of history, for instance, the teacher could read brief excerpts from two primary source documents, identify "facts" that were verified across both documents, and identify how the affiliations of the authors seemed to shape their interpretations of these facts.

Students then have opportunities to practice using these approaches to reading themselves, either verbally (through articulating what they are thinking to peers), or on paper (through writing their connections, clarifying questions, and visuals in the margins of a text). Ideally, teachers would provide such experience with multiple texts over a significant duration of time so students can have repeated practice with "thinking like a reader" as well as "thinking like a practitioner of social studies."

We argue that, much as novice students develop cognitive frameworks for approaching printed texts, so, too, they can develop cognitive frameworks for approaching a variety of multimodal texts, such as historical artifacts and a variety of visuals. Imagine, for instance, teachers thinking aloud as they interpret a newspaper article, political website, historical artifact, or other multimodal primary or secondary source through asking questions and making statements related to the topics in Figure 5.2, then giving their students opportunities to practice similar types of thinking.

Using frameworks such as these, teachers can model for students how they interpret multimodal texts according to discipline-specific frameworks, and give students practice with interpreting other multimodal texts using similar frameworks for thinking.

FIGURE 5.2. Framework for Interpreting Multimodal Texts

- What do I know about the creation of this text or object?
  - » What do I know about the social, economic, personal, or political circumstances that prompted its creation?
  - » Why was it made?
  - » For whom was it made?
  - » Whose interests and perspectives does it reflect or promote and whose interests and perspectives does it ignore?
  - » What are the assumptions that informed the creation of this object?
- Who are the authors of the text?
  - » What are their affiliations, or what groups do they belong to?
  - » How might these affiliations have affected their argument?
  - » How might somebody with different affiliations have presented the argument in a different way?
- What techniques did the authors use to convince others of their claims?
  - » What written techniques (e.g., metaphors, organizational patterns) did the authors use?
  - » What forms of representation did the authors use to prove their claims?
- What features of these representations prove the authors' point?
  - » Are there are any features of the representation (e.g., aspects of the photograph, aspects of the numeric table) that don't seem to prove the authors' point?
  - » Why might the authors have chosen these representations as opposed to other possible representations?
  - » How might people with a different perspective have represented or communicated the same issue differently? For instance, might they have used a different set of background colors, different subjects in the photograph, different variables in the graph, a different type of language, and so forth?
- How does the information in this source compare to or contrast with information in other sources?
  - » What facts in this argument or account seem to align with other sources?
  - » What facts in this argument or account seem to differ from the facts in other sources?
  - » What factors might explain this discrepancy?
- Is the evidence presented in this source (these sources) sufficient to prove this claim?
  - » If so, why?
  - » If not, what other sources could I consult?
- Would some types of representations (e.g., data displays of large-scale data sets) be better than other types of representations (e.g., photographs) for proving or explaining this claim? If so, which representations or collections of data sources would be best? Why?

CHAPTER INSIGHTS

Social studies is a diverse discipline, covering a range of overlapping subdisciplines such as civics, geography, economics, and history. Practitioners in these disciplines often regularly interpret a variety of modes in addition to writing, including visuals such as graphs, maps, drawings, and photographs, and also music or physical objects. In middle and high school classrooms, many teachers also require their students to produce embodied representations in this discipline as a means for fostering engagement and developing empathy.

The comprehension strategies detailed in this chapter,when applied in discipline-specific and authentic ways, can develop students' multimodal representational competence as well as their ability to evaluate texts according to a set of discipline-specific concerns. Moreover, MRC extends beyond the rigorous interpretation of texts; it also includes supporting students in producing and evaluating multimodal texts of their own. Although the interpretation of written texts remains central to the practice of social studies, people have long communicated opinions, arguments, and experiences through a variety of multimodal media as well, and these media should not be ignored as potentially rich sources of information, objects of study, and models for students' own multimodal texts.

CHAPTER 6

Reading and Representing Across the Content Areas

The preceding chapters of this book have shown that students in each discipline regularly interpret and produce a variety of texts that include, yet extend beyond, written texts. Often, these embodied, numeric, visual, and three-dimensional texts are not merely decorative add-ons that supplement students' understandings of written texts, but rather significant sources of learning in their own right. Students can use them to construct in-depth understandings of key disciplinary concepts much as they use written texts for the same purpose.

Consequently, we argue that conceptions of literacy instruction within each discipline should be extended to include comprehension instruction on a variety of representations, as well as opportunities for students to produce and evaluate a variety of representations of their own. Moreover, we assert that one goal of literacy instruction is the development of multimodal representational competence (MRC), which includes a broad set of practices related both to the interpretation and production of many types of representation.

Although we believe that content area literacy instruction, at its best, fosters multimodal representational competence, we do not mean to imply that literacy instruction is the same regardless of what discipline one is teaching. On the contrary, as students move from subject to subject in the course of a regular school day, the literacy practices within each discipline are often unique in at least two ways. First, each discipline tends to be communicated through different sets of representations. For instance, in our research we found that mathematics teachers rarely, if ever, asked students to interpret photographs, whereas social studies teachers frequently did. Consequently, rather than simply assuming that students will know how to use the right representation for the right purpose in each discipline, teachers and students should discuss which representations would be appropriate for communicating certain concepts, including which representations are better suited for some purposes but less so for others.

Second, even when students are interpreting the same types of texts, such as reading a graph in social studies and in mathematics, these acts of interpretation are embedded within distinctly different patterns of discipline-specific activity. In this book, for example, the mathematics students produced and interpreted line graphs in order to illustrate the patterns in an accompanying numeric table, whereas the social studies students interpreted a line graph in order to make inferences regarding why immigrants were more likely to come to the United States during certain eras. Because each discipline is characterized by a unique set of disciplinary activities, we argue that teachers can assist students in developing discipline-specific frameworks for interpreting and evaluating these representations through activities such as think-alouds and structured annotations. For instance, students of science can learn how to interpret three-dimensional models as a scientist would, as well as what constitutes a quality three-dimensional model, and students of English can learn how to interpret persuasive videos as an expert would, as well as what constitutes a quality persuasive video.

In other words, we assert that each discipline is communicated by a unique set of representations and a unique set of frameworks for interpreting and evaluating those representations, both of which students can learn so that they can be considered legitimate practitioners of that discipline. At the same time, however, we do not mean to suggest that students should be encouraged simply to reproduce "how things have been done." On the contrary, we argue that perhaps part of the reason that students disengage from some disciplines is because of the ways that these disciplines are communicated (Lemke, 1990).

Mathematicians and students of mathematics, for instance, often do not view photographs of people: In fact, they rarely view any images that look like any setting or object they would see in the everyday world. Instead, they commonly interpret more abstract shapes in decontextualized settings, such as a folded-out cylinder against a white background (O'Halloran, 2005; Wilson & Landon-Hays, in press). This decontextualization and lack of personalization also extends to written and numeric texts in this discipline. Students rarely read texts with first-person personal pronouns, such as "I came to the conclusion that . . . ," instead reading texts that present mathematical activity as relatively free from human influence, such as "The solution is . . . " (Rotman, 2000). This seemingly impersonal, decontextualized way in which mathematics is communicated may be one reason that some students do not feel an affinity for this discipline.

Accordingly, we would not recommend that mathematics teachers reproduce the status quo by exclusively teaching students to interpret, produce, and evaluate conventional representations, such as line graphs, equations, tables, and word problems—important as those may be to mathematical reasoning. This argument extends to teachers of other disciplines as well. For instance, some males do not like English/language arts when it seems too personal—when their teachers require them to express their feelings through poetry and when they project illustrations of characters and smiling photographs of literary authors, instead of more abstract scientific and mathematical images (Martino, 1999; Wilson & Landon-Hays, in press). In other words, given the diversity of students' preferences and backgrounds, any set of disciplinary representations may seem limiting to some learners if they are not allowed opportunities to produce "nonstandard representations" (Kozma & Russell, 1997) or "new representations" (diSessa, 2004). These representations are ones that might not typically be legitimized through textbooks or other published instructional materials, but they allow students to demonstrate their understandings in meaningful and creative ways nonetheless.

EMBRACING STUDENTS' DIVERSE REPRESENTATIONAL PRACTICES

Consequently, at its best, we envision instruction in multimodal representational competence as one that accounts for disciplinary practices and conventions as well as for students' preferred and valued methods of communicating. By "preferred and valued methods of communicating," we mean any method of communication through which students feel they can express their desired identities and group affiliations. For instance, some people may want to maintain identities as "mountain folk" through speaking Appalachian English (North Carolina Language and Life Project, 2008); therefore, science teachers could allow students to represent their understandings through using terms from their home language as well as from formal scientific language, an approach that has been shown to increase students' understandings of science (Warren, Ballenger, Ogonowski, Rosebery, & Hudicourt-Barnes, 2001).

As another example, we worked with a Navajo and Paiute student whose life mission statement was to "express himself in dance and not in words and writing" (Wilson & Boatright, 2011). Specifically, he preferred to communicate his self-proclaimed Native identity through grass dancing. To prepare for these dances, he frequently designed and beaded his own and others' head roaches, a form of headdress regalia for grass dancing, and he shared his drawings of these roaches with his peers and teachers at school. We can imagine mathematics lessons in which discussions of rotational symmetry or mathematical transformations (e.g., reflections) would be grounded in the types of reasoning that he used in order to make his head roach visually appealing. In other words, instruction on mathematical concepts and representations could begin with one of his preferred methods of communicating his identity: the head roach.

In a similar vein, Hill (2009), who worked with African American students in urban areas, found that hip-hop music was more than just rhythms and rhymes to himself and many of his students. Instead, he argued that "youth use hip-hop texts as complex sites of identity work" and he found that "rap music provided a useful hook that held their interest as [he] taught them the district-mandated curriculum" (pp. xvii-xviii). For some students, then, hip-hop language and movements are a form of expression that can be hybridized when combined with other disciplinary representations. For instance, we return to the assignment in which Alice asked her sixth-grade social studies students to compare how two groups of people spent their money on a daily basis. We can imagine that students who identified with hip-hop could use many of the same representations as before, such as photographs of affluent neighborhoods versus poor neighborhoods, but these representations could serve as the backdrop for embodied and spoken performances that highlighted economic disparities.

In this sense, we do not see instruction on representations as an either/or proposition by which students can either communicate like a historian *or* like a hip-hop artist; like a scientist *or* like mountain folk; like a grass dancer *or* like a mathematician. Instead, we envision classroom spaces in which students have opportunities to innovate by creating hybrid representations, which are valued as legitimate demonstrations of learning despite the fact that at times these representations may be deemed "nonstandard."

To be clear, we value standard representations as well: We know that they have been honed through trial and error over time and that the reason that they are accepted by each disciplinary community is because they are generally efficient at what they do and they enable people to communicate with each other. We know, for instance, that photographs or pictorial drawings may not help students solve mathematics problems to the same extent that more abstract images do, which is why mathematics teachers do not often encourage students to use the former types of visuals to solve problems (Edens & Potter, 2007). We know that scientists use line graphs to communicate relationships between variables because this format is clear, clean, precise, and understood by other scientists, which is why science teachers teach their students how to display data using this format.

At the same time, however, we would argue that allowing *only* "standard representations"—standard essay formats, standard line graphs, standard diagrams, and so forth—has disenfranchised many students who communicate at home and with their friends according to a different set of norms and standards. Many students may not feel that their identities can be expressed through standard or conventional forms of disciplinary language and representation (Wilson, Chavez, & Anders, 2012), leading them to decide that "this discipline is not for me." Consequently, while we value the ability to create standard representations, we likewise value the ability to produce new or alternative representations, ones in which students have more choices regarding what they say and how they say it.

REPRESENTATIONAL INSTRUCTION GROUNDED IN DESIGN

What might instruction in multimodal representational competence look like if it accounted for students' preferences as well as disciplinary conventions? We envision a type of MRC instruction centered around the concept of *design*, where students hold a central position as designers. In accordance with this position, students would have frequent opportunities to make decisions regarding how they wanted to build and express their understandings of disciplinary concepts. These decisions would enable students to draw from communicative resources they value, including those they use at home and with their friends in digital and embodied settings. Key to this type of instruction is the question: *How might I represent this?*

For instance, students can ask themselves questions such as these:

- How can I represent the causes of the phases of the moon?
- How can I represent these data showing daily changes in cloud shapes?

- How might I represent the causes and effects of global warming?
- What representations would persuade my audience to take action on this social issue?
- How might I represent this character's inner attributes (emotion, motivation, psychological conflict) at the moment he or she made this difficult decision?
- How might I represent aspects of my own identity, values, and upbringing in this personal narrative?
- How might I represent what I know about ratios?
- How can I represent the relationship between speed and time?
- What representations could help me solve this problem, and what are different ways I might represent my solution after I have solved it?
- How might I represent unemployment statistics in my community?
- How might I represent the experiences of the "new immigrants" to the United States at the turn of the 20th century?
- How might I represent my position on this political, ethical, or environmental issue? What representations might persuade my audience of the merits of my position?
- What types of representations would most fully prove my claims or support my argument regarding this social issue?

Instead of telling students to make a line graph, draw a diagram, or write a persuasive essay, these questions can require students to think more consciously about how they might use different representations for different purposes. Subsequently, they can compare their representations to their classmates' as well as to more conventional representations and discuss the merits and limitations of each, including which features had a powerful effect on them, which features might have been helpful, or which features might have been misleading. This approach has been shown to lead to increased understanding and engagement in learning across several disciplines (diSessa, 2004; Hubber et al., 2010).

As these examples also suggest, some questions may have the potential to engage students in broader forms of representational practices than others. It would probably be difficult for some students to use music to answer the question "What representations would help me solve this problem?" in mathematics. However, when mathematical activity is embedded in larger social issues like "How might I represent unemployment statistics in my community?" more opportunities arise for students to invent and use more diverse types of representation.

For example, students might represent the unemployment rate as a pie chart showing the percentage of the currently employed as compared to the currently unemployed, as a line graph showing changes in the unemployment rate over time, as a numeric ratio of unemployed men to unemployed women, as a numeric ratio of unemployed African Americans to unemployed Whites, and so on. In this case, music, artistic drawings, or video footage of somebody telling her unemployment story might help students to make an argument about unemployment in ways that embed mathematics in more diverse forms of representations, with students having more latitude to choose representations that align with their preferences and strengths. Part of teachers' instructional decisions, then, might at times entail selecting discipline-appropriate issues that can lend themselves to greater representational diversity and thus would enable students to have wider latitude in communicating using forms that are important to them.

In addition to allowing hybridized forms of representation, we imagine one final characteristic of classrooms that foster MRC : the encouragement of "representational play." We define representational play as informal experimentation with communicational forms that students enjoy, occurring within a classroom context wherein beautiful, fun, culturally diverse, and/or novel representations are routinely recognized and appreciated. We argue that representational possibilities continue to expand as technology expands, and that more people are presenting geographic, mathematical, scientific, and literary arguments in new and compelling ways that break with traditional formats. We further argue that experimentation with different representational forms has fueled innovation in every discipline. From authors' experimentation with new forms such as graphic novels or interactive hypertexts to miners' experimentation with cross sections as a means to represent layers of the earth, to mathematicians' experimentation with the connections between number and space, to cartographers' experimentation with thematic mapping—new methods of representation have enabled new ways of thinking and new types of activity in each field.

Accordingly, we argue that classroom environments that foster representational play can position students at the forefront of innovation as they consider how they might build and express their scientific, aesthetic, mathematical, or civic understandings using representational forms that transverse conventional disciplinary boundaries. Such classroom environ-ments actively encourage representational and communicative diversity. They value and legitimize nonstandard representations as potentially useful ways of knowing and communicating disciplinary concepts. They recognize students' preferred methods of communicating—whether through grass dancing, hip-hop, drawing, photography, or Spanglish—as valuable resources that do not run counter to disciplinary goals and tradi-tions, but instead can partner with traditional disciplinary forms of com-munication to produce richer and more engaged learning.

References

Achieve, Inc. (2013). *Next generation science standards.* Retrieved from: http://www.nextgenscience.org/next-generation-science-standards

Ainsworth, S. (1999). The functions of multiple representations. *Computers & Education, 33,* 131–152.

Ainsworth, S. (2006). DeFT: A conceptual framework for considering learning with multiple representations. *Learning and Instruction, 16,* 183–198.

Alvermann, D. E., & Wilson, A. A. (2011). Comprehension strategy instruction for multimodal texts in science. *Theory into Practice, 50,* 116–124.

American Association for the Advancement of Science. (2009). *Benchmarks for science literacy.* Retrieved from www.project2061.org/publications/bsl/online/index.php/

Applebee, A. N. (1974). *Tradition and reform in the teaching of English: A history.* Urbana, IL: National Council of Teachers of English.

Baron, C. (2012). Understanding historical thinking at historic sites. *Journal of Educational Psychology, 104,* 833–847.

Barton, K. C. (2005). Primary sources in history: Breaking through the myths. *Phi Delta Kappan, 86,* 745–753.

Bazerman, C. (1998). Emerging perspectives on the many dimensions of scientific discourse. In J. R. Martin & R. Veel (Eds.), *Reading science: Critical and functional perspectives on discourses of science* (pp. 15–28). London, England: Routledge.

Becher, T. (1989). Historians on history. *Studies in Higher Education, 14*(3), 263–278.

Beers, K. (2003). *When kids can't read, what teachers can do.* Portsmouth, NH: Heinemann.

Block, C. C., & Pressley, M. (Eds.). (2002). *Comprehension instruction: Research-based best practices.* New York, NY: Guilford Press.

Boal, A. (2006). *The aesthetics of the oppressed* (A. Jackson, Trans.). London, England: Routledge.

Brenner, M. E., Mayer, R. E., Moseley, B., Brar, T., Durán, R., Reed, B. S., & Webb, D. (1997). Learning by understanding: The role of multiple representations in learning algebra. *American Educational Research Journal, 34,* 663–689.

Brophy, J. (1996). Introduction. In J. Brophy (Ed.), *Advances in research on teaching: Teaching and learning history* (pp. 1–18). Greenwich, CT: JAI Press.

Brown, R., & Davis, G. (1990). Ages of Oscar-winning best actors and actresses. *The Mathematics Teacher, 83*(2), 96–102.

Buehl, D. (2009). *Classroom strategies for interactive learning* (3rd ed.). Newark, DE: International Reading Association.

Carr, R. E. (1961). *What is history?* Cambridge, UK: Cambridge University Press.

Christensen, L. (2000). *Reading, writing, and rising up: Teaching about social justice and the power of the written word.* Milwaukee, WI: Rethinking Schools.

Connolly, P., & Vilardi, T. (Eds.) (1989). *Writing to learn mathematics and science.* New York, NY: Teachers College Press.

Daniels, M. L. (2010). A living history classroom using re-enactment to enhance learning. *Social Education, 74,* 135–136.

Desoete, A., & Veenman, M.V.J. (Eds.). (2006). *Metacognition in mathematics education.* New York, NY: Nova Science.

diSessa, A. A. (2004). Metarepresentation: Native competence and targets for instruction. *Cognition and Instruction, 22,* 293–331.

diSessa, A. A., Hammer, D., Sherin, B., & Kolpakowski, T. (1991). Inventing graphing: Meta-representational expertise in children. *Journal of Mathematical Behavior, 10,* 117–160.

Duke, N. K., & Pearson, D. (2002). Effective practices for developing reading comprehension. In A. E. Farstrup & S. J. Samuels (Eds.), *What research has to say about reading instruction* (3rd ed., pp. 205–242). Newark, DE: International Reading Association.

Edens, K., & Potter E. (2007). The relationship of drawing and mathematical problem solving: "draw for math" tasks. *Studies in Art Education: A Journal of Issues and Research in Art Education, 48,* 282–298.

Fernandez, R. (1977). *Social psychology through literature.* New York, NY: Wiley.

Field, S., Labbo, D. L., Wilhelm, R. W., & Garrett, A. W. (1996). To touch, to feel, to see: Artifact inquiry in the social studies classroom. *Social Education, 60,* 141–143.

Fitzpatrick, C. (2011). A place for everything: Geographic analysis and geospatial tech in schools. *The Geography Teacher, 8*(1), 10–15.

Fogelberg, E., Skalinder, C., Satz, P., Hiller, B., Bernstein, L., & Vitantonio, S. (2008). *Integrating literacy and math strategies for K–6 teachers.* New York, NY: Guilford Press.

Foster, S. J. (2001). Historical empathy in theory and practice: Some final thoughts. In O. L. Davis, E. A. Yeager, & S. J. Foster (Eds.), *Historical empathy and perspective taking in the social studies* (pp. 167–181). Lanham, MD: Rowman & Littlefield.

Franks, A., Durran, J., & Burn, A. (2008). Stories of the three-legged stool: English, media, drama from critique to production. *English in Education, 40,* 64–79.

Gibson, J. J. (1979). *The ecological approach to visual perception.* Boston, MA: Houghton Mifflin.

Goodwin, C. (2000). Action and embodiment within situated human interaction. *Journal of Pragmatics, 32,* 1489–1522.

Graff, G. (1987). *Professing literature: An institutional history.* Chicago: University of Chicago Press.

Gray, E. M., Pinto, M., Pitta, D., & Tall, D. (1999). Knowledge construction and diverging thinking in elementary and advanced mathematics. *Educational Studies in Mathematics, 38,* 111–133.

Greenleaf, C. L., Litman, C., Hanson, T. L., Rosen, R., Boscardin, C. K., Herman, J., . . . Jones, B. (2011). Integrating literacy and science in biology: Teaching and learning impacts of reading apprenticeship professional development. *American Educational Research Journal, 48,* 647–717.

Hagan, S. (2007). Visual/verbal collaboration in print: Complementary differences, necessary ties, and an untapped rhetorical opportunity. *Written Communication, 24*(1), 49–83.

Hall, E. (1964). Silent assumptions in social communication. *Disorders of Communication, 42,* 41–55.

Halliday, M.A.K. (1973). *Explorations in the functions of language.* London, England: Edward Arnold.

Halliday, M.A.K., & Martin, J. R. (1993). *Writing science: Literacy and discursive power.* Pittsburgh, PA: University of Pittsburgh Press.

Hill, M. L. (2009). *Beats, rhymes, and classroom life: Hip-hop pedagogy and the politics of identity.* New York, NY: Teachers College Press.

Hoffman, M. H. G., Lenhard, J., & Seeger, F. (Eds.). (2005). *Activity and sign: Grounding mathematics education.* New York, NY: Springer.

Hubber, P., Tytler, R., & Haslam, F. (2010). Teaching and learning about force with a representational focus: Pedagogy and teacher change. *Research in Science Education, 40*(1), 5–28.

Jewitt, C. (2006). *Technology, literacy, and learning: A multimodal approach.* London, England: Routledge.

Jonassen, D. H. (1997). Instructional design model for well-structured and ill-structured problem-solving learning outcomes. *Educational Technology Research and Development, 45*(1), 35–52.

Jonassen, D. H. (2000). Toward a design theory of problem solving. *Educational Technology Research and Development, 48*(4), 63–85.

Kaiser Family Foundation. (2010). *Generation M2: Media in the lives of 8–18-year-olds.* Retrieved from: kff.org/other/event/generation-m2-media-in-the-lives-of/

Kastens, K. A., & Ishikawa, T. (2006). Spatial thinking in the geosciences and cognitive sciences: A cross-disciplinary look at the intersection of the two fields. In C. A. Manduca & D. W. Mogk (Eds.), *Earth and mind: How geologists think and learn about the earth* (pp. 53–76). Boulder, CO: Geological Society of America.

Knain, E. (2001). Ideologies in school science textbooks. *International Journal of Science Education, 23,* 319–329.

Knobel, M., & Lankshear, C. (2008). Remix: The art and craft of endless hybridization. *Journal of Adolescent & Adult Literacy, 52,* 22–33.

Kozma, R. B., & Russell, J. (1997). Multimedia and understanding: Expert and novice responses to different representations of chemical phenomena. *Journal of Research in Science Teaching, 34,* 949–968.

Kress, G. (2003). *Literacy in the new media age.* New York, NY: Routledge.

Kress, G. (2005). Gains and losses: New forms of texts, knowledge, and learning. *Computers and Composition, 22,* 5–22.

Kress, G. (2009). What is mode? In C. Jewitt (Ed.), *The Routledge handbook of multimodal analysis* (pp. 54–67). New York, NY: Routledge.

Kress, G. (2010). *Multimodality: A social semiotic approach to contemporary communication.* New York, NY: Routledge.

Kress, G., & van Leeuwen, T. (2001). *Multimodal discourse: The modes and media of contemporary communication.* London, England: Arnold.

Kress, G., & van Leeuwen, T. (2006). *Reading images: The grammar of visual design* (2nd ed.). London, England: Routledge.

Kuhn, D. (2010). Teaching and learning science as argument. *Science Education, 94,* 810–824.

Latour, B. (1987). *Science in action: How to follow scientists and engineers through society.* Cambridge, MA: Harvard University Press.

Lee, C. D., & Spratley, A. (2010). *Reading in the disciplines: The challenges of adolescent literacy.* New York, NY: Carnegie Corporation of New York. Retrieved from carnegie.org/fileadmin/Media/Publications/PDF/tta_Lee.pdf

Lemke, J. L. (1990). *Talking science: Language, learning, and values.* Westport, CT: Ablex.

Lemlich, C. (1909, November 28). Life in the shop. *New York Evening Journal.* Available online at www.ilr.cornell.edu/trianglefire/primary/testimonials/ootss_claralemlich.html

Lévesque, S. (2008). *Thinking historically: Educating students for the twenty-first century.* Toronto, Canada: University of Toronto Press.

Levstik, L. S. (2000). Articulating the silences: Teachers' and adolescents' conceptions of historical significance. In P. Stearns, P. Seixas, & S. Wineburg (Eds.), *Knowing, teaching, and learning history* (pp. 284–305). New York, NY: New York University Press.

Luke, A., O'Brien, J., & Comber, B. (1994). Making community texts objects of study. *The Australian Journal of Language and Literacy, 17,* 139–149.

Martino, W. (1999). "Cool boys," "party animals," "squids," and "poofters": Interrogating the dynamics and politics of adolescent masculinities in school. *British Journal of Sociology of Education, 20,* 239–263.

Miera, L. (1995). The microevolution of mathematical representations in children's activities. *Cognition and Instruction, 13,* 269–313.

Miller, J., & Saxton, J. (2004). *Into the story: Language in action through drama.* Portsmouth, NH: Heinemann.

Monaco, J. (1981). *How to read a film.* New York, NY: Oxford University Press.

National Council for the Social Studies. (1994). *Expectations of excellence: Curriculum standards for social studies.* Washington, DC: Author.

National Council for the Social Studies. (2013). *The college, career, and civic life (C3) framework for social studies state standards: Guidance for enhancing the rigor of K–12 civics, economics, geography, and history.* Silver Spring, MD: Author.

National Council of Teachers of English & International Reading Association.

(1996). *Standards for the English language arts.* Retrieved from www.ncte. org/library/NCTEFiles/Resources/Books/Sample/StandardsDoc.pdf

National Council of Teachers of Mathematics. (2000). *Principles and standards for school mathematics.* Reston, VA: Author.

National Governors Association Center for Best Practices & Council of Chief State School Officers. (2010). *Common core state standards.* Washington, DC: Author.

National Research Council. (2001). *Adding it up: Helping children learn mathematics.* Washington, DC: National Academies Press.

National Research Council. (2006). *Learning to think spatially.* Washington, DC: National Academies Press.

National Research Council. (2011). *A framework for K–12 science education: Practices, crosscutting concepts, and core ideas.* Washington, DC: National Academies Press.

National Science Foundation. (2010). *Earth science literacy: The big ideas and supporting concepts of earth science.* Retrieved from www.earthscienceliteracy. org/

Newton, P., Driver, R., & Osborne, J. (1999). The place of argumentation in the pedagogy of science. *International Journal of Science Education, 21,* 553–576.

Norris, S. (2009). Modal density and modal configurations: Multimodal actions. In C. Jewitt (Ed.), *The Routledge handbook of multimodal analysis* (pp. 78–91). New York, NY: Routledge.

North Carolina Language and Life Project. (2008). *Appalachian English* [Video file]. Retrieved from www.youtube.com/watch?v=03iwAY4KlIU

O'Halloran, K. L. (2005). *Mathematical discourse: Language, symbolism, and visual images.* New York, NY: Continuum.

Orion, N., & Ault, C. R., Jr. (2007). Learning earth science. In S. K. Abell & N. G. Lederman (Eds.), *Handbook of research on science education* (pp. 653–687). Mahwah, NJ: Lawrence Erlbaum.

Osborne, J. (2002). Science without literacy: A ship without a sail? *Cambridge Journal of Education, 32,* 203–218.

Paulos, J. A. (1996). *A mathematician reads the newspaper.* New York, NY: Basic Books.

Peirce, C. S. (1991). *Peirce on signs: Writings on semiotic.* Chapel Hill, NC: University of North Carolina Press.

Perry, N., & McGuirk, R. (2013, April 6). Antarctic ice samples: What do they say about global warming? *Christian Science Monitor.* Retrieved from www. csmonitor.com/Science/2013/0406/Antarctic-ice-samples-What-do-they-say-about-global-warming

Prain, V., & Tytler, R. (2012). Learning through constructing representations in science: A framework of representational construction affordances. *International Journal of Science Education, 34,* 2751–2773.

Pressley, M. (2002). Metacognition and self-regulated comprehension. In A. E. Farstrup & S. J. Samuels (Eds.), *What research has to say about reading instruction* (3rd ed., pp. 292–309). Newark, DE: International Reading Association.

Rosario-Ramos, E. (2010). *Reading the socio-political: The interaction between comprehension and critical literacy.* Paper presented at the National Reading Conference, Fort Worth, TX.

Roth, W.-M. (2004). What is the meaning of meaning? A case study from graphing. *Journal of Mathematical Behavior, 23,* 75–92.

Rotman, B. (2000). *Mathematics as sign: Writing, imagining, counting.* Stanford, CA: Stanford University Press.

Rudwick, M. J. S. (1976). The emergence of a visual language for geological science, 1760–1840. *History of Science, 14,* 149–195.

Rylant, C. (1992). *An angel for Solomon Singer.* New York, NY: Orchard Press.

Samuels, S. J., & Farstrup, A. E. (2011). (Eds.). *What research has to say about reading instruction* (4th ed.). Newark, DE: International Reading Association.

Schneider, J. J., Crumpler, T., & Rogers, T. (Eds). (2006). *Process drama and multiple literacies: Addressing social, cultural, and ethical issues.* Portsmouth, NH: Heinemann.

Schoenbach, R., Greenleaf, C., & Murphy, L. (2012). *Reading for understanding: How reading apprenticeship improves disciplinary learning in secondary and college classrooms.* San Francisco, CA: Jossey-Bass.

Seely-Flint, A., & Laman, T. (2012). Where poems hide: Finding reflective, critical spaces inside writing workshop. *Theory Into Practice, 51,* 12–19.

Shanahan, T., & Shanahan, C. H. (2008). Teaching disciplinary literacy to adolescents: Rethinking content-area literacy. *Harvard Educational Review, 78,* 40–61.

Siegel, M. (1995). More than words: The generative power of transmediation for learning. *Canadian Journal of Education, 20,* 455–475.

Smagorinsky, P., & O'Donnell-Allen, C. (1998). Reading as mediated and mediating action: Composing meaning for literature through multimedia interpretive texts. *Reading Research Quarterly, 33,* 198–226.

Soares, L. B., & Wood, K. (2010). A critical literacy perspective for teaching and learning social studies. *The Reading Teacher, 63,* 486–494.

Spinelli, J. (1990). *Maniac Magee.* Boston, MA: Little, Brown.

Stoessiger, R. (2002). An introduction to critical numeracy. *Australian Mathematics Teacher, 58*(4), 17–20.

Suiter, M. C., & Stierholz, K. L. (2011). Data and primary source documents for social studies classrooms from the Federal Reserve Bank of St. Louis. *Social Education, 75*(2), 92–95.

Timmins, G., Vernon, K., & Kinealy, C. (2005). *Teaching and learning history.* London, England: SAGE.

van Leeuwen, T. (1999). *Speech, music, sound.* New York, NY: St. Martin's Press.

van Leeuwen, T. (2005). *Introducing social semiotics.* London, England: Routledge.

Warren, B., Ballenger, C., Ogonowski, M., Rosebery, A. S., & Hudicourt-Barnes, J. (2001). Rethinking diversity in learning science: The logic of everyday sense-making. *Journal of Research in Science Teaching, 38,* 529–552.

Which country has the best brains? (2010, October 8). *BBC News Magazine.* Retrieved from www.bbc.co.uk/news/magazine-11500373

Wilhelm, J. (1997). *You gotta BE the book: Teaching engaged and reflective reading with adolescents.* New York, NY: Teachers College Press.

Wilson, A. A. (2010). The nature of texts used in five academic disciplines. In R. T. Jiménez, V. J. Risko, D. W. Rowe, & M. K. Hudley (Eds.), *The 59th Yearbook of the National Reading Conference* (pp. 154–170). Oak Creek, WI: National Reading Conference.

Wilson, A. A. (2012). How changes in representation can affect meaning. In R. Andrews, E. Borg, S. B. Davis, M. Domingo, & J. England (Eds.), *SAGE handbook of digital dissertations and theses* (pp. 427–441). Thousand Oaks, CA: SAGE.

Wilson, A. A. (2013). Actional-operational modes in earth science and implications for literacy instruction. *Science Education, 97,* 524–549.

Wilson, A. A., & Boatright, M. D. (2011). One adolescent's construction of native identity in school: "Speaking with dance and not in words and writing." *Research in the Teaching of English, 45,* 252–277.

Wilson, A. A., Boatright, M. D., & Landon-Hays, M. (2014). Middle school teachers' discipline-specific use of gestures and implications for disciplinary literacy instruction. *Journal of Literacy Research, 46,* 1–29.

Wilson, A. A., Chavez, K., & Anders, P. (2012). "From the Koran and Family Guy": The expression of identities in English learners' digital podcasts. *Journal of Adolescent & Adult Literacy, 55,* 374–384.

Wilson, A. A., & Landon-Hays, M. (in press). A social semiotic analysis of instructional images across disciplines. *Visual Communication.*

Wineburg, S. (1991). On the reading of historical texts: Notes on the breach between school and the academy. *American Educational Research Journal, 28,* 495–519.

Wineburg, S., & Grossman, P. (2000). Scenes from a courtship: Some theoretical and practical implications of the interdisciplinary humanities curricula in the comprehensive high school. In S. Wineburg & P. Grossman (Eds.), *Interdisciplinary curricula: Challenges to implementation* (pp. 57–73). New York, NY: Teachers College Press.

Wineburg, S., Martin, D., & Monte-Sano, C. (2011). *Reading like a historian: Teaching literacy in middle and high school history classrooms.* New York, NY: Teachers College Press.

Yilmaz, K. (2007). Historical empathy and its implications for classroom practices in schools. *The History Teacher, 40,* 331–337.

Yore, L. D., & Hand, B. (2010). Epilogue: Plotting a research agenda for multiple representations, multiple modality, and multimodal representational competency. *Research in Science Education, 40,* 291–314.

Index

About the Authors

Amy Alexandra Wilson is a former middle and high school teacher who currently teaches content area literacy at Utah State University. Her interests include culturally responsive content area literacy instruction for adolescents.

Kathryn J. Chavez is a secondary curriculum specialist in the Tucson Unified School District. Her teaching experience in middle school classrooms and work with adolescent second language learners guides her research in the LRC department at the University of Arizona.